THE
OLD SOUL'S GUIDEBOOK

AINSLIE
MACLEOD

THE

OLD
SOUL'S
GUIDEBOOK

Who You Are, Why You're Here,
&
How to Navigate Life On Earth

SOUL WORLD PRESS®
SEATTLE

Because your mind, body, and spirit are inseparable, your soul's lifetimes of experience affect every aspect of who you are—from your personality and beliefs, to your talents and fears. Without knowing who you were, you can never truly know who you are.

— AINSLIE MACLEOD'S SPIRIT GUIDES

ALSO BY AINSLIE MACLEOD

The Instruction

The Transformation

Heal Your Past-Life Fears [Audio]

Past-Life Regression [Audio]

ISBN 978-1-7329255-0-2 (Paperback)

Except where noted, all names and identifying details have been changed to preserve anonymity.

First printing edition 2019

Soul World Press

PO Box 1604, Vashon, WA, 98070

soulworld.com

ainsliemacleod.com

To my wife, Christine. You truly are the love of my life.

CONTENTS

PROLOGUE

YOUR SOUL'S COSMIC JOURNEY

*Y*our soul is on a journey with one overarching mission: to truly understand all there is to know about being human. This is why you've been coming here to the Physical Plane for millennia, and why your many incarnations have given you the opportunity to grow by experiencing life in every part of the world.

In your earliest incarnations, the lives you lived were simple. You hunted, fished, fell in love, reproduced, and came to grips with being in a solid body from within the safety of the tribe. But when you were ready, you began to look beyond the village walls to make the world your school.

Your soul's thirst for growth has constantly impelled you from within to keep exploring. Over the span of thousands of years, you've marched with mighty armies, built monuments to your gods and kings, and sought ways to give your life meaning. You've lived lives of wealth and power, and many more of drudgery, brutality, and powerlessness.

You learned about justice and compassion through suffering and hardship, and taught younger, less experienced souls powerful lessons that you embodied from firsthand knowledge.

Your soul saw every experience, however harsh, as an opportunity for growth. You loved and lost, but in doing so, learned the importance of love. You killed and were killed, and that taught you to value the sanctity of life.

As an old soul, you've been visiting and revisiting this world for something like five or six thousand years. You've explored different genders and race. You've been gay, straight and everything in between. You've worn every color skin. And throughout your long and often arduous trek, your choices have always been made to ensure a well-rounded education.

Now here you are, back on the planet once more. The question is why? To answer that, it's essential to know what led to your decision to be here again.

Without knowing where you've been, you can never truly know where you're going. And everything—from the circumstances of your birth, to your dreams and aspirations—is influenced by your soul's past.

In fact, I don't think I can stress this enough: Everything you are—your personality, your beliefs, your aspirations, your talents, your fears—is entirely the result of your soul's many lifetimes of experience.

How do I know all this? For over two decades, I've used my psychic abilities to explore the world of the soul. I've written two books, taught many classes and workshops, and worked with thousands of individual clients. But I wasn't always a spiritual teacher and psychic. For most of my life, I was just a regular Muggle. I considered myself an atheist and flew my skeptic flag with pride—and even a smidgen of arrogance. I used to think life was just a series of random events, completely devoid of meaning. And even when psychics told me I was one of them, I thought they were making it up.

As a child growing up in Scotland, I saw ghosts, had vivid premonitions, and could always tell when someone was lying. And what seems crazy now is that I never for one single moment thought any of those experiences pointed to my being psychic. Clinging obstinately to my "rational" view of the world, I put everything down to coincidence or just "one of those things."

Yet, and this may seem odd for someone who had no belief in a world beyond this, I was drawn to psychics. I told myself I was visiting them to debunk them. Truth was I really did—on a soul level at least—believe. It just took me a long time to overcome my deeply-held beliefs in, well, nothing. At least, nothing beyond what I could see and touch.

Then the spirit world whacked me over the back of the head with a metaphysical 2x4, and finally got my full attention.

In the space of a few months, two significant events rocked my world and woke me up from my slumber. In my early 40s, I took a flight from the East Coast to San Francisco, planning to stay for a few weeks. Just hours after my arrival, I heard the words a psychic had spoken to me ten years earlier while I was still living in the UK: "You're going to end up in California. There's nothing you can do about it." He was right. What I thought would only be a short trip turned into permanent relocation.

Then, a few months later, on a trip to Hawaii, I ran into my uncle in a bookstore in Kauai (which was something of a surprise since he'd been dead for over a decade). He appeared slightly to my right, looking just as he had in life, and was there for about a second. And he gave me a message. He said that in his capacity as a spirit guide, he wanted to work with me.

Those two events changed the course of my life, and were what I needed to accept my destiny and embark on my current path. A few weeks after my brief encounter with my uncle I made my first attempt to communicate with him on the other side. I was blown away to find I actually could.

Through my Uncle John, I was introduced to a higher level of guides, ones whose entire purpose is to help those of us on this plane make the most of our time here. My spirit guides are souls who have completed all their lives on the Physical Plane, and now devote themselves to doing what their name suggests.

Communicating with those in spirit was far from easy. For the first year, trying to hear my spirit guides was like listening to a faint radio signal from another planet. It would take me an hour to do what would now take five minutes. Then I hit on a method I still use today. It allowed me two levels of communication, increased my level of accuracy, and made everything so much faster.

Three years after I began working with my guides, I was ready to go professional. All I had to deal with was my discomfort with actually being known as a psychic. My first career was as an artist, and even after it had been years since I'd last put pencil to paper I'd still tell people that was my job. Someone told me once that psychics were top of a list of least respected professions, sandwiched between mob boss and televangelist. And though I'd met some truly amazing psychics in my time, I knew that with that particular profession being so full of frauds it would be hard to avoid being lumped in with them.

Over time, I gradually threw off the "Reluctant Psychic" label I'd chosen for myself, and with strong encouragement from those on the other side, jumped in with both feet. On my birthday, one year, when my children excitedly presented me with personalized plates for my new car, I had a momentary feeling of "Oh Gawd!" but it didn't last, and I certainly didn't want to disappoint them by being ungrateful. (So, if you see a car with license plates that read P5YCH1C, say hello—that's me: The Proud Psychic.)

My first book, *The Instruction: Living the Life Your Soul Intended,* gave me the first opportunity to share what I feel are the most incredible discoveries into human nature. The actual method, The Instruction itself, was something I channeled about a year before writing the book. I've been using the system for years now, and I continue to learn more about how it works, how different elements interact with one another, and how it explains what each of us is doing here.

Three years after publication of *The Instruction*, I wrote *The Transformation: Healing Your Past Lives to Realize Your Soul's Potential*. It describes the purpose of reincarnation and the incredible power of past-life healing as way to achieve a state of higher spiritual consciousness.

The Old Soul's Guidebook is my third work. My reason for writing it is to share my experiences and knowledge to help you make the very best of your life. I would love for this to be a book you refer to as a way to enhance your life's journey through greater awareness of your purpose, know how to transcend obstacles in your path, and recognize important karmic lessons and significant spiritual connections that are part of your soul's plan. In the same way my work with my spirit guides continually deepens my understanding of the soul's purpose, I hope you'll regularly come back to the book as your voyage unfolds.

As well as helping you to better understand your life's purpose, I offer *The Old Soul's Guidebook* as an antidote to the plethora of misinformation that has muddied the waters of genuine spiritual insight in recent years. It's surprising, for example, how many people think everything is meant to be (it's not), or that if life isn't working out for you then you're being punished for something you did in another incarnation. Such beliefs can be dangerously disempowering.

Though my discoveries into the nature of the soul and its purpose are far from scientific (I don't do double-blind tests or conduct methodical experiments), this book is not based on supposition or conjecture. My understanding of the soul and its purpose comes directly from the source which is, of course, my spirit guides.

The spirit guides' decision to choose me for this work was based, in part, on my passion for the subject and my talents for both intuition and empathy, developed—as are all talents—over many lifetimes.

My specialty, my field of interest, and my obsession is the soul and how it influences every single aspect of human life. I've spent the larger part of every day for the last 20 years talking with my spirit guides. To the very best of my understanding, what I share is the way things are.

YOUR SOUL'S PLAN

Your soul's journey has lasted for thousands of years and spanned many lifetimes. Unlike your conscious mind and your body, your soul doesn't actually die after each incarnation. Instead, it travels between lives to another dimension, to what's known as the Astral Plane. Before each lifetime, the Astral Plane is where it plans all the significant lessons it wants to investigate during its upcoming adventure on earth. And when each incarnation is over, it's where it goes to process what it learned.

Your life, far from being a series of random events, is carefully planned long before you first make your appearance in this world. Your soul always seeks to evolve, and for that reason, it chooses whatever circumstances it thinks will offer the biggest lessons. To make sure that you get the most out of each incarnation, it creates a road map for the life ahead. This "life plan" includes a list of places to go, people to meet, lessons to learn, and missions to be accomplished. Your life plan is your destiny.

It's crucial to understand that your destiny is not something that's "out there" somewhere. It's not a distant goal like taking a Mediterranean cruise when you retire. Your destiny is not a mystery that will eventually be revealed after decades of navel-gazing and personal development classes. It's what is happening now.

Fulfilling your destiny means doing what's consistent with your life plan in every moment. All you have to know is what's actually in your life plan. Which, surprisingly enough, is not that hard to find.

You might imagine that with all the planning that happens on the Astral Plane, you simply have to come to earth, follow the directions, and all will be well. Yet how many of us can say we really know who we are or why we're here, or that we're doing exactly what we feel we should be doing?

If your soul is aware of what's in your best interest, where you should be, and what you should be doing, why is it so hard for your conscious mind to get it? Why do so many of us stumble blindly through life unaware of our purpose? Is your destiny hidden from you for a reason? Is it some kind of arcane secret, its mysteries accessible only to those with some kind of esoteric knowledge?

Your destiny is *not* a secret. The universe never seeks to confound you by making your life's purpose mysterious and elusive. In fact, it's quite the opposite. If you know what to look for, your destiny is staring you right in the face.

As an old soul, your journey is in full swing. And life won't always be easy. You might be dealing with difficult parents, raising challenging children, struggling with an unfulfilling job, having difficulty finding or keeping your soulmate, coping with deep, inner uncertainties, or living with the effects of less than ideal decisions, disappointments, limiting beliefs, physical ailments, and a host of other things that keep the journey interesting.

How you deal with life's challenges is, to a large extent, up to you. Your life plan is your route map to help keep you on track, but you have unlimited free will. You can take your life in any direction you want. (That's why it's so important to understand your destiny.) It allows you to navigate your own path with confidence, knowing what's consistent with your soul's plan for this incarnation.

Again, your destiny is not some intangible holy grail that you might, if you're fortunate, discover sometime before you die. As long as your goals are consistent with your life plan, you can manifest your destiny right now.

My destiny has led me to write this book to help you uncover your life's purpose and guide you towards a more purposeful and fulfilling incarnation. I'm not a therapist. And I'm not a guru, either. I'm not here to tell you how to live your life. Your decisions are always yours to make. You're the one leading the expedition. I'm simply here to help you by sharing what I've learned from my spirit guides.

I've included some of my own personal story in the book. I do so to make the point that though I've faced my share of challenges during this incarnation, I've learned how to roll with the punches, and I've done it through the work I now offer to others. I may be a teacher, but that doesn't mean I'm not still a student.

I also offer numerous anecdotes from client sessions. All the examples are chosen to help you better understand your soul's purpose, and to empower you. In most cases, names and identifying details have been changed out of respect for privacy.

My sincere expectation is that you'll find a deeper understanding of who you are and why you're here in the pages of this guidebook. I hope it serves as a road map and compass to help you better navigate your journey on Earth, and that you use what you discover within these pages to make this your best incarnation ever.

I wish you bon voyage!

BEFORE WE BEGIN

Throughout the book, I reference aspects of your soul's life plan as described in my book, *The Instruction.* When I refer, for example, to a desire for Immortality, capitalizing the word "immortality" indicates that the desire is a specific term related to the soul's life plan.

Also, as the proud father of a transgender child, I've learned to be respectful in my use of pronouns. For that reason, I use "they/them/theirs" in place of "he/him/his" or "she/her/hers" where appropriate (no matter how often autocorrect tries to tell me otherwise).

Each chapter contains an exercise to help you explore your soul's purpose in this life. I encourage you to spend time on these exercises, and even journal about what you uncover. Through writing, you'll reach a deeper place of understanding.

IN A ROOM OF A HUNDRED PEOPLE...

In these pages, you'll find short sections entitled *In a Room of a Hundred People.* These are brief examples of the various idiosyncrasies that have their origins in past lives. When I encounter one during a session, I'll often say to my client, "If I put you in a room of 100 people, you'd be the only one who..." (Like when I told a client she'd lost her teeth under torture in a past life, and she revealed that she still has all her baby teeth at the age of 45.)

My purpose in sharing these examples (besides lending weight to my hypothesis that *everything* is past-life related) is to show you how even the oddest quirks can be explained when you take reincarnation into account.

I

THE JOURNEY BEGINS

1

FROM FEAR TO ETERNITY

THE PURPOSE OF REINCARNATION

*I*f you're an old soul (and if you're interested in this topic, that's a given), then what are the signs? How can we pick you out of a crowd? To answer that, we first need to understand the part reincarnation plays in making you who you are.

For your soul, it's been a long, frequently exhausting, and even dangerous mission. Since first leaving the safety of the spiritual realm several thousand years ago, your soul has undertaken a quest for new experiences that would make the voyages of the Starship Enterprise look uneventful.

And now, here you are, back on the Physical Plane for the umpteenth time, in a brand-new body with a whole new set of goals and missions to accomplish.

Your conscious mind, your body, and your soul are inseparable. Wherever your soul goes, there go you. Your destiny is entwined. Without mind or body, your soul is helpless. Without your soul, you are nothing. You need each other to survive.

It's no exaggeration to say that your soul makes you who you are. It's responsible for your motivations, your desires, your fears, and your personality. How you see the world is through your soul's eyes. Its centuries of experience influence your beliefs and behavior in every way.

But what is the soul? Where does it come from? How do you know if you've even got one?

Your soul is what gives you consciousness. (And when I say "you," I'm talking about the mind and body that house your soul.) You and your soul were joined at birth, so to speak, when your physical and spiritual selves commingled. That was the first time you'd both met, but because your soul's memories are infused with your conscious mind, it was more like a reunion than a first encounter.

Human souls originated some 55,000 years ago, at a time when our species was mostly still living in Africa. It was then that Homo sapiens underwent a radical shift in consciousness—one that would alter our entire future. Our giant leap resulted in us becoming the creatures of virtually unlimited reason and creativity that we are now.

Your own personal soul hasn't actually been around that long, though. Maybe something like five or six thousand years at most. That's roughly how long it takes for any soul to get everything done here on the Physical Plane, or to go from life number one to life one hundred and something. (The average is around 120.)

There are three planes of existence that are important to know about. The first is the Physical Plane, which is where you are now, and the second is the Astral Plane, where your soul goes between lives. The third, the Causal Plane, lies somewhere beyond the Astral Plane. Your soul started out, like every other soul, on the Causal Plane. It's where your journey began, and where it will eventually end.

Prior to becoming part of the Causal Plane, your soul split off from an even greater universal consciousness. That's when it joined a large number of souls who chose to share the voyage with you. These souls are your spiritual family and play an important part in your personal evolution.

After first leaving the Causal Plane, you won't see home again until you complete all your lives and reunite with your soul family. The closest you'll get in the meantime is the Astral Plane. That's where you'll go to plan upcoming lives and process the ones you've just completed. In human terms, your time spent on the Astral Plane between lives can be measured in months or decades. It all depends on what particular opportunities your soul is looking for. It might wait a long time to be incarnated in a specific location with a certain pair of parents.

A CHILD'S DESCRIPTION OF REINCARNATION

Many children can recall being between lives on the Astral Plane. Jenny, my client's eight-year-old daughter, had the following conversation with her father once at bedtime:

"Before you're born," she said, "You sit around with all the people you're going to know in your next life. You talk about all the things you want to do, then you say, 'Now we're going to do it for real'.

After that, you can't go back. I chose you as my dad," she said, "And I love you and you're the best daddy in the whole world. But, you know, next time, I might be the mom and you can be the son."

THE IMPULSE TO EVOLVE

The process of choosing a new incarnation takes time. You want to make sure you get the timing right, find the perfect location, and figure out the various agreements you'll make with other souls to help you achieve whatever it is you're trying to get done.

So, what's the point of all this? Why does your soul go to such an effort? Wouldn't it be a lot easier just to stay on the Causal Plane and not come here in the first place?

Just like a shark has to keep moving forward to survive, your soul has to keep learning in order to grow. And your mind and body are obliged to go with it.

If your soul didn't have this impetus to evolve, you'd still be sitting around the Paleolithic campfire chipping arrowheads from flint and worshipping the sun and moon, just as you did in your earliest lifetimes.

Since those primitive Stone Age tribal beginnings, you've had many incarnations. Some were mundane and uneventful, while others were jam-packed with excitement. A few were marred by events so traumatic they impact you to this day. Each one has contributed to making you the unique individual you are now.

Every incarnation is chosen for the opportunity to evolve. You choose your parents, your siblings, your friends, and your partners. You select specific lessons to learn, for reasons we'll explore in this and later chapters. You also want to seek out members of your soul family at every opportunity.

Thanks to reincarnation, you have multiple opportunities to develop talents and abilities and to use the Physical Plane as your earthly school. It's here you learn to work with others and to build each lifetime on the foundation of the last.

As your soul ages, it goes from a place of fear to one of love. This shows up in how you see the world. Younger souls tend to be more fearful and are suspicious of those whose beliefs are different from theirs. Older souls, with more experience of the world, are generally more accepting.

Understanding the age of your soul is vital to really knowing who you are and why you're here. Which is why it's one of the first things I look at in a psychic reading, why the subject of soul ages is the first chapter of my book, *The Instruction*, and why it's something we'll explore in more detail in Chapter Two.

Thousands of years of travel on planet Earth have broadened your mind. As an old soul, you're likely to consider yourself more spiritual than strictly religious. And even if you do express your spirituality through religion, you're no longer driven to impose it on others. Your political and social views will reflect your higher level of compassion, and I'd expect you to respect nature and the world you live in.

Centuries ago, you lived in a world where petty thieves were publicly branded or even dismembered. Women were burned for sorcery. Human beings of all ages were abducted and sold into slavery.

And though terrible injustices still exist, your consciousness has elevated to a point where you'd never dream of condoning or turning a blind eye to such acts of cruelty.

As an old soul, you recognize, through your own bitter experience, that we're all connected and that we all deserve to be treated with dignity.

To ensure maximum growth, you've run the gamut of all that life can offer. You've been male, female, gay, straight, asexual, non-binary, and more. You've been rich and poor, loved and unloved, a bold adventurer, and a retiring homebody.

You've fought and died in wars, explored new frontiers in the arts and sciences, and learned, often through painful experiences, about the darkest aspects of human selfishness, arrogance, and brutality.

You've been a priest, a farmer, a baker, a teacher, a soldier, a blacksmith, a hunter, an artist, a miller, a merchant, and a magistrate. You've been a father, a mother, a son, a daughter, a servant, a slave, and a prostitute. It's all part of the human experience.

When it gets to the Physical Plane, your soul doesn't shy away from throwing itself into the fray. It wants to roll up its sleeves and get involved in life.

Though the circumstances of your many lifetimes may seem random, they're the results of choices your soul made, with the help of spirit guides, while still in its spiritual home-away-from-home on the Astral Plane.

SPIRIT GUIDES

When I first began working with spirit guides, it wasn't totally clear where my specialty would lie. I had no interest in talking to those I describe as "freshly dead," or being a medical medium. I was, however, already interested in channeled material, curious about human beliefs and behavior, and obsessed with understanding the soul's purpose.

I liken spirit guides to opinions and certain body parts—we all have them. Mediums and most psychics communicate with guides on the Astral Plane, ones whose purpose is to help with more prosaic, everyday questions, to offer reassurance, and to communicate with those who have passed.

My spirit guides reside on the Causal Plane, which gives them access to the big picture. They know everything about you.

From their elevated vantage point, Causal Plane spirit guides see who you are, who you've been, and why you're here. They know the details of the intricate agreements you created as part of your life plan before you incarnated.

They understand what it is you're trying to achieve in this lifetime. And they have one overarching purpose: to guide you on your soul's journey.

But before settling into my niche as someone who uses past lives to help people find their purpose in this life, I had to experiment a little.

I helped find a couple of missing children (not as dramatic as it sounds, since they'd simply run away from home, and it was clear they'd be back soon), but I was uncomfortable with what might happen if I ever had to tell someone their child was dead.

The spirit guides and I agreed that finding missing people was not to be my specialty. Then a friend called and said he'd lost a necklace he'd picked up in Vietnam. I told him it was stuck between a duvet and a nightstand in a guest room.

To his amazement (and mine, I have to admit), he found a necklace exactly where I described, but it was a different one that he'd bought on a previous trip. I asked my spirit guides if finding missing objects would be a good business to go into. They didn't seem particularly excited.

I also helped get rid of a malicious entity that was causing mayhem in a Seattle business. The premises had previously been owned by a deceased TV chef who had faced multiple allegations of sexual abuse involving teenage boys.

I cleared out the bad energy and all was well, but the spirit guides made me agree before going that this would be the one and only time I'd ever be a Ghostbuster.

My spirit guides seemed to enjoy letting me explore different psychic avenues before nudging me on the path that took me to where I am now. And as time passed, my "purview," as they like to call it, narrowed down to what had interested me in the first place.

My role is to act as an emissary or messenger, and deliver what I get as accurately as possible. My spirit guides communicate with humor, gentleness, and respect for free will. Unless someone is being abused or their life is in danger, they'll rarely tell anyone what to do. Their purview is to guide, not coerce.

SPIRIT GUIDES AND ANGELS

One frequent question I get asked is, "What's the difference between a spirit guide and an angel?" The answer is that it really comes down to semantics.

When I first met my spirit guides I asked, "How do I address you?"

They said, "Spirit guides."

I use the term spirit guides, but you can call them angels or whatever you like.

———————

My spirit guides and I have worked with thousands of people in one-on-one sessions, and in groups—both online and in person. As you'll discover, I have a fascination with the ways in which our past lives make us who we are.

After doing this work for many years, and after countless hours of discussion with my spirit guides, I've become convinced that reincarnation truly explains everything.

Reincarnation has long been associated with Hinduism, Buddhism and contemporary spirituality. But a survey conducted by the Global Research Society and the Institute for Social Research in 2011 showed that 51% of the world's population believes in reincarnation, a number I actually find shockingly low given the ample evidence for its existence.

Is there proof of reincarnation? I believe so. You can, at least, see convincing evidence for it if you know where to look. All talents, for example, are past-life abilities.

Any aptitude you have is there because you've had the chance to develop it over many lifetimes. If you have a gift for music, for example, it's because you've had a lot of practice over the centuries.

In my work, parents often tell me about how their kids reveal their past lives through casual comments like, "When I was in my big body..." or "When I used to be your mom..." Sometimes they'll describe places they've been and things that they've done in other lifetimes.

We'll hear a lot more of this as time goes on, and the concept of reincarnation becomes a more acceptable topic for polite conversation.

PRACTICE MAKES PERFECT

Through social media, it's likely you've come across examples of children with remarkable abilities, like the four-year old pianist who could give Rachmaninoff a run for his money. These little geniuses are simply picking up where they left off in previous incarnations.

We don't switch species from one lifetime to the next. From your first life to your last, you'll be human. You're not going to come back as Mehitabel the cat or Archie the cockroach.

But animals also reincarnate, which means a cat, a dog, or a horse that you've known in a life before this may share your life now. And because their lives are shorter, they might join you more than once in a single lifetime.

My feline companion, Lily (who is curled up on my lap as I write these words), was my childhood pet, Tiger. We go back thousands of years together, and that made it easy to recognize one another when we met at the rescue center.

OUR FURRY SOULMATES

Dogs often choose to reincarnate in the same breed they've been in earlier incarnations.

I told a client once that I'd try to guess the breed of her dog from their past life together.

"He used to catch rats in a warehouse in London's Limehouse district," I said, "So I'd expect he's a terrier."

"He's actually a rat terrier," she replied. (And she was the merchant who owned the warehouse.)

Every life you've had has been as a human. And every life was just as real as this one. And that's the problem. Your soul has carried all sorts of memories from earlier lives into this one.

In my opinion, the most exciting thing about reincarnation is this: There's virtually no problem you have, whether it's procrastination, a fear of public speaking, low self-esteem, or even constipation, that can't be healed, improved upon, or completely eliminated, by understanding what took place in your past lives.

Let me give you an example.

SPIRITUAL HEALING

A few years ago, when I first worked with my client, Kerry, my spirit guides said she would become known for speaking in public. Having struggled with a stutter for 40 years, the idea seemed absurd to her at the time.

"I've lived with a stutter all my life. As my mom tells it, when I was five-years old, the stutter came home from school with me.

"The stutter is always just below the surface," Kerry said. "I can feel the emotions around certain words; mainly proper nouns. And yes, that includes my own name! I can't tell you how many times I've introduced myself to someone only to hear 'Are you sure that's your name?'

"Once, during my teenage years, a teacher unknowingly caused complete mortification. Our class stood in a circle, taking turns reading the lines of a play.

"By the time my turn came around, I was so anxious I thought I might faint. I remember the room swimming and my heart racing. I seriously thought I was going to pass out.

"I couldn't form a coherent sentence. My teacher's response was, 'Can't you read?' After that, I developed a fear—no, a dread —of public speaking.

I even found it hard to order dinner in a restaurant, especially if we were at a large table with a bunch of friends. My friends knew that was why my husband would order for me.

"Not being able to verbally express yourself, especially when you have so much to say, has a way of making you feel so small and ashamed. I couldn't even give a toast to thank everyone at my own wedding."

Then Kerry was offered the opportunity to host a radio show with her friend Tiffanie. "You can imagine how that made me feel!" she said. "When we recorded the first show, all I felt was gripping, painful fear. I stuttered, I stammered, I cringed.

"Basically, I was that teenager back in high school. The day after that first recording session, my co-host wanted to listen back to the show, but I just couldn't do it. The thought of hearing myself was just too painful."

A few months later, during a session Kerry had with me, my spirit guides revealed the source of the problem. While she waited patiently on the other end of the phone, they told me about a significant past life in 17th Century France.

She'd been a young man who'd stolen clothing from a laundry and had ended up being beheaded. One detail I uncovered was that after his arrest, the militia broke his left foot to prevent him escaping.

The memory of this injury shows up in this life as a bone protrusion and arthritis at the site of the past-life injury. I knew immediately that the trauma I was seeing would have made a lasting impression on her soul. "This is huge," I told her.

At his execution, he was jeered at and ridiculed by the crowd, and the memory of that humiliation carried through into Kerry's present life as a fear of Judgment.

Stuttering is a manifestation of her soul's deep-seated anxiety about what others say or think about her. The trigger was any situation that made her soul feel judged again.

My spirit guides confidently told Kerry that the next time she went in front of a microphone, her stutter would be gone. She was skeptical. "I'm really fond of you," she laughed, "But that's just too much to expect!"

It didn't take long for her to find out if she actually would experience the past-life healing my guides promised. "The very next morning, we did a show. I didn't stutter. I didn't stammer. I wasn't quiet. In fact, I said every thought that came to mind. I was relaxed, and I had a blast!

"Afterwards, Tiffanie, my cohost, looked at me and said, "What the f**k was that?!!" (She's usually very sweet and proper —no curse words.) I explained what had happened in my session with you and we both laughed and hugged."

For Kerry, the healing work we did together has been life changing. She wrote to me recently saying, "I owe you so much. I'll say it again, I am in awe of what you and your spirit guides do. Thank you from the bottom of my heart."

(In April of 2018, my wife, Christine, and I had the honor of being interviewed by Kerry and Tiffanie on their show. If Kerry stuttered, I didn't notice it.)

Because I see this kind of transformation on such a regular basis, you'd think it would become routine for me. But it still blows me away each time, and continually reminds me of the incredible power of past-life healing.

You might imagine that with someone being an old soul with scores of lifetimes behind them, they'd be reaching a point of perfection by now. And, in many ways, you'd be right. It just doesn't always look that way.

When I tell a client they're an exceptionally old soul, their first response is usually along the lines of, "If I'm such an old soul, how come I have so many fears and anxieties?"

It's a good question.

2

SO YOU THINK YOU'RE AN OLD SOUL?

HOW REINCARNATION SHAPES YOUR WORLD

*I*n this culture, most people want to be younger than they are. But when it comes to the soul, that's when everyone wants to be older. We look at a baby and say, "She seems like such a wise old soul." We associate wisdom with being an experienced soul, and use the term old soul when talking about Gandhi or Martin Luther King, Jr.

But what does it mean to be an old soul? Can you really identify an old-soul baby? What are the markers of an old soul? If you're an old soul, how do you compare to younger souls? How do you get to be an old soul? And if you're such an old soul, how come you haven't reached some place of perfection?

Your soul age is based on how many times you've incarnated on earth, and what you've learned from being here.

Your soul is impelled, as are all souls, to evolve. And it will keep coming here to the Physical Plane until, as a very old soul, it feels it has learned all it needs to know about being human.

So, if there are old souls in this world, it means there have to be young souls, right? Of course. But it's important to remember that no matter how old you are now, you were once a young soul.

There's a tendency for older souls to look down on young

souls. It's hard not to, and I still find myself getting exasperated and being less than charitable towards younger souls when they act out (particularly those young hooligans who run riot in the corridors of power).

But you don't—or at least shouldn't—get mad at a child when they fail to understand how to do something you, as an adult, take for granted: *"I can't believe you don't know how to drive the car—you're seven-years old!"*

And the same principle applies to young souls. You need to recognize their limitations. But that doesn't, of course, mean condoning bad behavior, whether it comes from a child or an inexperienced soul.

FINDING YOUR PLACE IN THE WORLD

Your soul had to start somewhere. There was a moment when you came into this world like a newborn—wide-eyed and, in the case of your soul, scared.

Imagine walking into a party where you don't know anyone or how to act. That's what it was like for you in your first few lives. You didn't understand the world, everything was unfamiliar, and everyone else seemed to be more confident than you. It was a scary place.

Arriving on planet Earth for the first time, however, your soul immediately began seeking out members of its soul family to avoid the feeling of being thrown into the deep end all alone.

In your soul's very earliest incarnations, your biggest lessons were all chosen to help you get used to being human. With few or no past-life fears to overcome, karma to balance, or talents and abilities to be built upon, you chose lives in small tribal communities where you could come to grips with basic survival issues.

You just wanted to live quietly while you found out how language, intellect, and your reproductive organs worked.

You put your unquestioning trust in others you assumed were

wiser. You fought battles because you were told it was the right thing to do. It was easier to follow orders than to question them.

You required a strict moral code or set of religious laws to teach you how to behave. You believed that only your god, or gods, were worthy of worship.

Like all very young souls, you embraced the certainty of fundamentalism and appreciated not having to face questions that might have threatened your limited worldview.

Because you still had to learn that no soul is intrinsically better or worse than any other, you might have been the perpetrator of injustice as often as you were the victim.

The young soul person you used to be was not intrinsically bad. You just lacked the experience to make good choices. But that was a long time ago.

You've had many lifetimes since then. To say you've changed would be an understatement.

SIGNS OF MATURITY

As a young soul, you saw yourself and those with whom you identified—your family, your church, and your community—as those you could trust.

Everyone else was 'the other.' You were uncertain about foreigners and people who were differently pigmented, and you were suspicious of those who worshiped the wrong deity.

As a man, you might have considered women, even those closest to you—your mother or child—as second-class citizens.

But when you went from being a young soul to an old soul (roughly around halfway through your soul's many incarnations), your perspective shifted.

A newfound ability for introspection allowed you to question more deeply. And that led your conscious mind to connect more strongly with your soul and its many lifetimes of experience.

OLD SOUL EMPATHY

One significant sign that you're an old soul is a greater than average degree of empathy. The deeper connection between your soul and conscious-self allows you to recognize the humanity in others. For this reason, it's unusual for any old soul (except one that's spiritually blocked, or heavily influenced by their parents or their culture) to support the death penalty or the use of torture.

An old soul like you will tend to be more peaceful. Through personal experience, your soul has learned that war solves nothing, and that killing or dying for your country, your religion, or for access to resources, is pointless.

When you graduated from being a young soul, it was as if a mist cleared, or a blurred picture came into focus. In the young-soul cycle of lives, the world gradually became a less scary place to be. And when you made the transition to the old-soul cycle, you became much more accepting of those unlike yourself, and generally more concerned with the wellbeing of others.

Very young souls, the ones who are still a long way from learning that we humans are all connected, tend to be more rigid in their outlook. They mistrust those they don't understand, such as members of a different faith, individuals or groups who don't conform to their idea of what's normal (like trans people or gays), or anyone who doesn't think the way they do. (Not to say that old souls can't be bigoted too.)

Many young souls are drawn to the safety that religion brings them. Because of this need to feel safe, they surround themselves with like-minded, kindred spirits. In the United States, this is the reason for mega-churches, where tens of thousands gather to have their beliefs validated. And in the Middle East, it's one reason why millions flock to Mecca every year for the Hajj.

Older souls tend to be less strict in their beliefs. They often describe themselves as spiritual, not so much religious. Even if old souls do belong to a church, they don't necessarily accept all the dogma that goes with it. And they don't fear having their beliefs challenged. (Predominantly old-soul Unitarians don't shun those who leave the church in the same way as predominantly young-soul Mormons.)

One of the most telling markers of a very young-soul community is that conformity is expected and monitored. Young souls use the law to enforce morality and, depending on where and when in history they happen to be, they'll crack down on non-believers, gays, drug users or drinkers, "uppity" women, people of color, and anyone with the temerity to challenge the status quo. Not surprisingly, no one in such an environment wants to stand out because, if they do, they'll be viewed with suspicion or even targeted for reprisals.

THE LEFT/RIGHT DIVIDE

Reincarnation and politics are inseparable. Where you stand on any issue, from a woman's right to choose to the death penalty, is not simply a question of upbringing, education, or environment. It's directly related to your soul's age and experience.

As I pointed out earlier, young souls are like children and teens. They're inexperienced and can be somewhat naïve. Their lack of worldly experience means that although they may not have all the answers, they don't know what they don't know. As a result, their beliefs can be rigid, their convictions unshakable, and they often think they know it all. The world is an easier place to navigate when everything is black and white.

Old souls are more akin to adults and seniors. Their perspective is the result of lifetimes spent accumulating wisdom in all parts of the globe. They've known what it's like to be on the receiving end of injustice, discrimination, and the abuse of authority often enough to embody the lessons learned.

In the modern world, the most obvious sign of this difference between young and old souls can be seen in the political arena. Those on the right wing tend to be younger souls, while those on the left wing are generally older. The age of a person's soul is never more evident than at the ballot box.

Souls with the least experience see the world as a scary place. They always look to strong leaders to save them from the boogieman du jour. Historically, there's always been someone who's going to steal their jobs, corrupt their children, or destroy their way of life. And there's always going to be a charismatic leader who promises to keep them safe.

In the past, the threat came from Communists, pot-smoking hippies, gays, pacifists, feminists, liberals, and abortion providers. In more recent times, it's been Al-Qaeda, ISIS, gun-control advocates, undocumented immigrants, environmentalists, refugees, and even transgender people who might use the "wrong" bathroom.

Young souls look up to those in authority. Throughout history, they've unquestioningly followed military leaders and explorers, certain in the wisdom of those in authority (as long as their leaders claim to support their causes or beliefs).

Their need to belong helps galvanize them when there's an enemy to rally against, whether it's the leader of another faith, an entire race or religion, or anyone who marches to a different drummer. They love to get behind a cause, though they don't want to be confused by nuance. Abortion is bad and easy to get fired up about. But income inequality is too complex an issue to deal with.

As the soul ages, its perspective changes. Multiple incarnations in different cultures teach it that the street sweeper in Delhi is no better or worse than the CEO in Chicago. Its evolutionary path takes it to a place where it recognizes the soul beneath the skin.

DRACONIAN SENTENCING AND THE SOUL

When it comes to law and order, young souls' thirst for safety means they want to lock 'em up and throw away the keys. Their fear of "the other" causes them to throw compassion and fairness out of the window, too.

That's why many people in younger-soul countries and communities end up doing hard time for what are essentially victimless crimes like smoking pot, prostitution, vagrancy, or for being unable to pay fines for trivial offenses.

Let me stress again that young souls are not inherently worse than old souls. Your three-year old might flush your iPhone down the toilet and blame the dog. But you recognize that your child is still a good person. Young souls frequently do things no old soul would. It doesn't mean they're bad—just inexperienced. And of course, there was a time when you were just like them.

THE TEN SOUL AGES

For you to become an old soul, you have to pass through ten distinct levels, or soul ages. From start to finish, this process takes about 5,000 to 6,000 years. With infant mortality being high, you might have incarnated more often than the average 120 times, but the spirit guides usually only count the lives where you made it past the first year or two.

Though there are just ten soul levels, you'll have experienced multiple lives at each stage. You might have taken twenty lifetimes to work your way through Level 4, but just six to cruise through a later level. It all depends on lessons learned—or not.

At the end of Level 5, at roughly the halfway point, you transitioned from being a young soul to an old soul. It was then that your ability to empathize with others took a great leap forward, thanks to a newfound ability for self-examination.

Your introduction to the Physical Plane at Levels 1 and 2 were simply about getting your feet wet. Level 1 lives are usually spent in communities that you, as an old soul, would find crushingly boring. Each day would look much the same as the last.

LEVEL ONE

I asked my spirit guides for a contemporary example of a Level 1 soul. They told me about a young woman who works in a fish factory in Angola. The factory is brand new, and she seems happy in her work. Her main recreation is watching soap operas on TV (which is a way to understand how to interact with other humans), but, as a result of their influence, she over-emotes, just like the people on the shows. Her ambitions don't extend beyond finding a husband and having children. It is, however, a good life to get started with.

LEVEL TWO

An example of a Level 2 soul is a logger in the Andes. The big lesson at Level 2 is cooperation, and being part of a team is exactly what this young man needs. Like the woman in Angola, he's content with his job. He gets to spend time with his family as well as his work buddies, which is, again, an opportunity to learn about being human. Being Level 2 means he has no desire to take a position of authority. It's quite likely he'll still be doing the same job twenty years from now.

LEVEL THREE

An Amish family in rural Pennsylvania is typical of souls at Level 3. The lessons at this stage are all about community and belonging. Everyone in the family feels a part of something bigger. They don't want to stand out—that need for conformity I spoke about earlier is a big deal at this stage—and they feel secure basing their behavior on the literal word of God.

An inability to trust those they don't understand keeps groups like the Amish insular and makes it hard for outsiders to gain access. Typically, Level 3 souls, wherever they are, marry within their religion or culture.

LEVEL FOUR

By Level 4, however, souls want to expand their horizons, so they begin to venture more into the outside world. Yet, that world is full of old souls whose values and beliefs seem very different. Out of fear, Level 4 souls create strict (often religious-based) laws to punish those who don't conform.

In *The Instruction,* I wrote about how these inexperienced souls look up to Level 5 souls, as long as they feel those souls share their values. Sadly, this makes them easy prey for those who have no problem exploiting this naivete. It also goes a long way toward explaining why so many people vote against their own social and economic interests.

Their capacity for hypocrisy can be noticeably greater than that of other soul ages. Sometimes, their hypocrisy makes the headlines, as in the case of the anti-gay, family-values preaching, married, Ohio State House Representative who was caught having sex with men in his office.

LEVEL FIVE

The consciousness of the United States—and the world as a whole—is predominantly that of Level 5. Therefore, Level 5 is often assumed to be normal.

Level 5 souls are not innately unkind or selfish, but their lack of any real concern for the condition of those less fortunate than themselves helps to maintain a gulf between rich and poor that would be the envy of a Roman emperor or a 19th Century robber baron.

These dynamic souls are drawn to power, and that's the reason most world leaders are Level 5. Often justified by principles such as manifest destiny, the divine right of kings, or American exceptionalism, these souls believe the planet and its resources are theirs to use as they please.

The big lesson for Level 5 souls is exploration, but it can easily slip into exploitation. Look at how they colonized the New World, and you'll get the idea. It probably won't surprise you to learn that Wall Street banks and multinational corporations are generally soul-crushing Level 5 institutions.

At the end of Level 5 comes the flip that takes all souls from an external to a more internal focus. You end one life as a Level 5 and come into the next with your eyes open in a way that simply wasn't possible before.

LEVEL SIX

Like a teenager entering adulthood, Level 6 souls see themselves and others as part of a larger whole. They form unions, guilds, sororities, and fraternal organizations to help themselves and others like them, as they turn their focus inwards in an attempt to better understand the world. Unlike younger souls whose motivation to be a part of something bigger than themselves is tribal, Level 6 souls want change.

With introspection being the big lesson, a Level 6 soul will toss and turn at night, questioning their ethics, concerned about the way they treated a co-worker earlier in the day, and whether or not they should have left a bigger tip at dinner.

Many great philosophers are, or were, Level 6 souls trying to figure life out. Polysyllabic vocabulary and complicated theories reflect the complexity they observe in the world around them.

LEVEL SEVEN

At the next stage, Level 7 souls share a greater than ever desire to see a better world. With the growing awareness that they'll have to come back here in future lifetimes, they recycle, contribute to good causes, and would seriously consider buying a Prius for environmental reasons (even if they do end up with an Infiniti).

Souls at this age compare themselves to others, and try to keep up with the Joneses, the Patels, or the Perez's, and have a heightened concern about what people say or think of them. They might trade in their Infiniti (or Prius) every couple of years just to show they're not economically inferior.

Level 7 is a time of creativity and innovation. Leonardo da Vinci, Michelangelo, most of the Impressionist artists, Bill Gates, Thomas Edison, and Alexander Graham Bell are, or were, in that zone. They are the beneficiaries of a residual Level 5 drive, combined with the Level 7 introspection needed to forge new ground.

LEVEL EIGHT

As the soul graduates to Level 8, it once again explores lessons in cooperation and reciprocity, as it did when it was much younger. But, unlike young souls who help out their immediate neighbors or community, they form cooperative ventures—non-profit businesses or foundations—and they like meetings.

BEING INVOLVED

I once asked a Level 8 client how many committees she sat on. The answer was six. Most old souls run the other way at the mere mention of the word "meeting." Level 8 souls, on the other hand, enjoy the protocol, the interaction, and the opportunity to make a difference.

Level 8 souls are all about people. They love to belong. They run farmers' markets, homeless shelters, crisis centers, and join gyms and golf clubs for the social life as much as the exercise.

In countries like Britain, they don't just go to a pub, but have a "local;" somewhere they'll meet other "regulars," for whom the company is as much an attraction as the beer.

When the Rainbow Warrior—Greenpeace's flagship—puts itself between a harpoon and a whale, we have Level 8 souls to thank. They have the energy and passion to get involved in ways other souls generally don't.

LEVEL NINE

The first question my Level 9 client, Beth, had for me was, "What is my life's purpose?" The answer was, "Healing." Which is not unusual for a Level 9 soul. She's a physician, but like most Level 9 doctors I work with, she has also studied other modalities. She's a trained acupuncturist and is gradually moving into the area of integrative medicine.

Like all Level 9 souls, Beth wants to constantly heal, improve, recover, and generally be all she can be. Typical of those at her soul age, personal freedom is of great importance to her.

She meditates, does Pilates, and has learned to ride a Harley Davidson. Without Level 9 souls, the whole mind, body, and spirit industry would collapse overnight. (And I'd lose approximately 65% of my clientele.)

Oprah Winfrey is a Level 9 soul, as are many of the amazing people she interviews on subjects related to the soul and personal development.

Level 9s bring sensitivity to an often-harsh world. Their compassion and empathy cause many of them to avoid watching the news, as they find it distressing.

Should they choose to get involved in politics or human rights issues, however, they can become unstoppable in their fight for justice and equality. That concern about the well-being of others continues into the last phase of life on earth at Level 10.

LEVEL TEN

After something like 6,000 years on the Physical Plane, living in every part of the world, and having been in every color of skin, Level 10s are highly compassionate and accepting of others. And, having been around the block so many times, some are exhausted and ready for retirement.

I asked Margie, a client who called me after a five-year hiatus, "Do you remember your soul age from your last session?"

She said, "Your spirit guides told me if I was a horse they'd have to take me out and shoot me." (Fortunately, old souls usually have a good sense of humor.) She's actually at the end of Level 10, getting ready to exit this world for the last time.

Level 10 souls can be a little eccentric and usually choose activities that give them pleasure or meaning over those that might be more lucrative. Many are self-employed, as they don't generally like being told what to do. They rarely thrive in the corporate world.

EXERCISE: HOW OLD IS YOUR SOUL?

Now it's time to figure out just how old a soul you are. This list is a reminder of the signs and markers of each of the ten soul ages. Don't overthink this exercise. Simply choose the level that resonates most strongly with you.

- **Level 1:** Isolation, Simplicity, Naivety
- **Level 2:** Fundamentalism, Nationalism, Discrimination
- **Level 3:** Church, Conformity, Conservatism
- **Level 4:** Morality, Aspiration, Hypocrisy
- **Level 5:** Ambition, Materialism, Exploitation
- **Level 6:** Social Justice, Uncertainty, Introspection
- **Level 7:** Complexity, Creativity, Innovation
- **Level 8:** Activism, Liberalism, Sophistication
- **Level 9:** Spirituality, Self-improvement, Healing
- **Level 10:** Altruism, Inertia, Compassion

When you know your soul age, you can better understand how you fit into the world. And you'll find that when you see others in terms of their soul age, you'll become more compassionate, recognizing that their beliefs and behavior are the result of their experience.

You'll start to notice, too, that it's not only individuals who reveal their soul ages through their beliefs and behavior. Families, businesses, and even whole countries reflect their predominant soul age.

The ultimate reason for going through all your many incarnations is not to become a shining beacon of perfection. It is simply to get to a point where all the major lessons associated with being human have been embodied.

You don't stumble across these lessons by accident. To make sure you get the growth your soul is always seeking, it does everything it can to help you follow your life plan, the map it created for this particular voyage. This life plan, as I pointed out earlier, is your destiny.

Every single one of us has a destiny. Does that mean that you're a prisoner of your life plan, a passenger on a runaway train, helpless to change course or alter the future? Let's find out.

3

FREE WILL OR DESTINY?

FOLLOWING YOUR SOUL'S LIFE PLAN

*I*s your job your destiny? Is travel your destiny? Is chronic illness your destiny? Is poverty your destiny? Sexual satisfaction? Theater? Writing? Being a healer? Playing the piano? Having children? Being childless?

Is crossing the Antarctic by dogsled to reach the South Pole your destiny? No? How do you know?

Unless you're the one person reading this who says, "I've always wanted to travel to the South Pole by dogsled," then you'll know it's not something you're here to do. And you'll know it because it won't resonate with you in any way.

When I told my client, Lucy, that she was meant to be a dancer, it resonated right away. "I've always wanted to be a dance teacher," she said. She will, because it's her destiny, and she knows it. Like many of my clients, however, she just required a little validation.

Deep down, you know your destiny. That's why, when a doctor tells you you're pregnant, you respond with, "Woo-hoo!" or "Oh, no!" (Or, perhaps, if you're a guy, "I demand a second opinion!") Your destiny is always at your fingertips. It's often just a question of knowing where to look.

And if you have a destiny, what then of free will? Is your conscious self the hobo hitching a ride on your soul's caboose, trundling blindly along some prearranged path? Or do you have the ability to shape your journey and choose different destinations along the way?

I'd like to give you an example from my own life to demonstrate the way free will, destiny, and intuition intersect. The principles apply, of course, to you and every other old soul.

As the adult child of an alcoholic father, I did what such people often do. I drifted into destructive relationships without ever recognizing the pattern I was in. In my 30s, I spent four stressful years in London with someone who was both alcoholic and mentally ill. And when I moved to the United States to be with my next partner, the dysfunction in her life was reassuringly familiar. As she would later put it, "You came from a chaotic background into my chaos and thought it was normal."

She was right. And after five years together, our relationship was in tatters. Sometimes I'd bail out to get away from the violent rages and the distressing sight of someone I loved drinking herself into a blackout every night. I'd wake up alone in a room in Motel 6 wondering how the hell everyone else but me seemed to find normal relationships.

Despite all the craziness, our meeting was destiny, in that we had a soul connection and a spiritual agreement to be together. But no agreement, even one forged between two souls on the Astral Plane, is carved in stone. At a particularly low point, destiny appeared, free will kicked in, and in the space of a few days, everything changed.

My old friend Bettina, a gifted psychic in London, called me at my home in Atlanta and told me, "You need to get out before you get hurt."

The next day, I got a call from my friend Frances, who told me she was leaving her home in San Francisco for a month-long vacation in the U.K. After hanging up the phone, I thought, "Wait, what's she doing with her flat?" I called her back immediately, but she'd gone. It took me 24 hours, but I finally tracked her down just as she was arriving at a friend's house in England. She was happy to let me use her place, and a week later, I was in San Francisco.

As I mentioned earlier, years before I moved to the States an English psychic, David Walton, had told me, "You're going to end up in California." But I'd filed his observation away, and never really thought about it.

What I didn't know at the time was that moving to California was an essential part of my life plan. I had total free will, but the universe would conspire to get me there. All I had to do was seize the opportunities as they came along.

Being in the relationship with my soulmate had also been destiny. But sometimes things just don't work out as expected. The conversation with Bettina was destiny, and acting on her advice was using free will.

The call from Frances was also destiny, but recognizing I had the opportunity to go to San Francisco was using my intuition, and calling a dozen people to find her was, once again, free will.

I never once thought about deliberately fulfilling David Walton's prediction. Ending up in California required doing nothing more than acting on intuition and seizing opportunities that felt right.

There was, by that time, a soul-to-soul agreement with my wife to split up. No soul will tolerate being abused for very long, and no soul wants to hurt another. Going our separate ways allowed me to embark on my career as a psychic and, several years later, led to my ex's recovery thanks to the 12-Step Program.

My agreement with Frances was, on a soul level, designed to get me to the West Coast. She didn't consciously know it, but she was acting as what my spirit guides call an angel (a principle I'll talk more about later). Her decision to call me was instigated by her spirit guides and designed to help me in a time of crisis.

Significantly, when I chose to head west, everything began to flow. At the time, I was a commercial illustrator. On my first day in San Francisco, a client I'd known in New York called to offer me work. He'd moved to a branch of his company there and was pleasantly surprised to find I was able to discuss the job in person. Being on the spot led to a lot more work, including drawing the character Chester Cheetah for Frito Lay.

When you learn to balance free will and destiny, you develop a kind of synergy between you and your spirit guides. It takes both to make your life plan work. They can set up the opportunities, but they can't make a phone call, book an air ticket, or relocate. That sort of thing is your job.

As I said in the Prologue, your destiny is *not* a secret. It may be a little tricky to access, but the universe is not out to make your life any harder than it needs to be. It also bears repeating that your destiny is right there in front of you if you know where to look, by which I mean being aware of what goals are consistent with your life plan, recognizing opportunities when they're presented to you, and using your intuition to make appropriate decisions.

Your life plan is a map, but you have the free will it takes to follow, deviate from, or ignore it at any time. You have the ability to make unlimited choices. Your free will means you're never a victim of your destiny, but a co-creator. Your soul and your conscious-self make a powerful team. One has the map, the other the ability to take action.

DESIGNING YOUR LIFE PLAN

Let's take a closer look at what's in your life plan. We know you choose your parents and other relationships. You choose places to live and visit, too. But what else? Do you choose your school or college? Do you choose your career? And what of those times when life really sucks? Do you choose to break your arm? Suffer abuse? Lose your dad when you're just a kid?

Your soul doesn't ever deliberately put you in harm's way. It tries at all times to guide you to avoid life's pitfalls. But that doesn't mean it won't choose situations where you're going to face some pretty stiff challenges. It never says something like, "Let's find out what it's like to lose a leg in a car crash," or "I want to be a sexually abused child for the lessons I'll learn." It doesn't work like that. The Physical Plane is a chaotic, dangerous place. Bad stuff will find you. The challenge is avoiding it.

However, sometimes your soul will choose extremely trying circumstances. In this harsh world, hardship is inevitable. When misfortune is seen ahead of time—when the soul knows before entering your body that the life won't be easy—the choice will be for the lessons offered. That's when a soul will say, "Being an AIDS orphan in Uganda is going to teach me some very important lessons this time around." It may be a tough path to choose, but no one can exist on Earth without a soul. Someone has to do it.

In planning your life, your soul will decide such things as what culture you'd like to experience, and whether or not you're going to want an education beyond high-school level. It'll look at careers it feels will help fulfill its life plan. Then it will select appropriate locations to help make it all happen.

SUPPORT FROM THE UNIVERSE

In a session with a client, I'll be asked something like, "Is going back to school to become a social worker the right path for me?" When the answer from the spirit guides is, "one hundred percent supported," what they mean is that your soul is excited by it, your spirit guides are behind it, and it's consistent with your life plan. "One hundred percent supported" means you've got a green light and two thumbs up.

You might think that your decision to go to a particular school or take a certain job is just about the education or the career opportunity. But what lies behind all your major life decisions is your soul's compelling need to reunite with members of its soul family —the kindred spirits with whom you left the Causal Plane for the grand tour of the physical world.

Though your journey began on the Causal Plane, your life plan was created by your soul with the help of spirit guides on the Astral Plane. One day, your soul will return to the Causal Plane when it feels sufficiently enriched by all its experiences. Until then, it will end each life on Planet Earth with regular rest and recuperation on the Astral Plane.

Before coming into this life, your soul spent a lot of time deciding on all the major lessons to learn, people to meet, places to go, and fears to be healed.

Its choices included that of its family, which, for obvious reasons, can come as a bit of a shocker. When I tell someone that they were born into their particular family by mutual agreement, the usual reaction is something like "What the heck was I thinking?"

In choosing the circumstances of its birth, your soul was actually thinking, "What circumstances do I need to help me evolve?" Your soul is nothing if not pragmatic, and it selected your family for its own personal development.

SUCCESSFUL LIFE PLANS

Creating a successful life includes finding the right people to help you complete your chosen lessons. Many of my clients come to me looking for their soulmates. Miranda was ready to meet hers, so I helped her narrow down what she was looking for.

I gave her a technique to help bring the right guy into her life (see the end of Chapter Nine for the specific exercise), and told her he'd turn up shortly— which he did—in the form of a fellow named Tom.

Miranda and Tom are old friends, meaning they're from the same soul family, the group of souls who all incarnated at the same time. They've been together in previous lifetimes many times before, and have a strong spiritual motivation to be with one another again. Their relationship is karmic, which simply means they need to balance certain past-life experiences.

I USED TO BE YOUR GRANDMOTHER

In my work, I'm always hearing about how children say things like, "When I was an old man..." or "I drowned and left my body..."

My client Judith told me how her 3-year old granddaughter had casually announced to her mother, "I used to be your grandmother Dorothy."

"Who is Dorothy?" I asked Judith.

"Dorothy was my ex-husband's mother," she said.

"It looks like Dorothy's back to heal some negative stuff from her last life. Was she difficult?"

"She was always extremely polite when other people were around. But when we were alone, she'd tell me, 'You're not good enough for my son!'"

Reincarnating as Judith's grandchild gives Dorothy a chance to balance the negative karma she created in her last incarnation by being a more loving presence in this one.

Shortly after they met, I was telling Miranda about her past lives with Tom. "He used to be your mother," I said.

Miranda laughed. "It's so embarrassing! I've called him Mom several times. The last time was yesterday when I said, 'Sounds good, Mom.' I felt like such a dork!"

In a recent lifetime, Tom had been the mother and lost the child that's now Miranda. Their souls are drawn to one another, in part to allow Tom to nurture the child he lost. But one of the other major reasons for being together turned out to be a mutual desire to travel.

In a later session, Miranda wanted to know where she and Tom had been together in their many past lives.

I said, "You had a life in Montreal where you were both engineers."

"I've always wanted to go to Montreal," she said. "And I love the smell of big machines and cars."

"You had another life in Iceland…"

"I'm obsessed with Iceland!"

"You were both academics in Italy with an interest in astronomy."

"We're fascinated by astronomy and quantum physics!"

"You lived in Paris in the early 20th Century. It was the life where he lost you."

"I've always been in love with the world of Coco Chanel!"

And so it went on. All the places they've been in the past are ones their souls want them to visit again. She and Tom are now married and planning trips to all the locations that hold special meaning for them both.

Your experience of life on Planet Earth is enhanced enormously when you learn to recognize your destiny, understand how your past lives affect you now, and use your free will to make the decisions to keep your spiritual journey moving forward.

SPIRIT GUIDES AND FREE WILL

As an old soul, you might be having difficulty finding or keeping a soulmate, or living with the effects of less than ideal decisions. One of the challenges for me as a psychic is finding ways to offer someone guidance without interfering with their free will, especially when someone is suffering as a result of their choices.

When someone asks, "Should I leave my partner?" I'll tell them, "Unless you're being abused, the spirit guides will never tell you what to do. My guides and I are not in the business of breaking up or saving relationships. We simply help you understand where your soul is so you can make appropriate choices."

To answer the $64,000 question regarding a relationship, I'll ask my spirit guides about the lesson in love. Technically, there's no single lesson in love that brings a couple of souls together, but if the spirit guides say the lesson is over, then one or both souls are done. It means there's no glue left to hold the relationship together.

Sometimes a couple whose lesson in love is over will agree to continue more as roommates than lovers, or choose to stay together, perhaps for financial reasons.

If the spirit guides say the lesson in love is *not* over, then there's still potential. Sometimes, however, without action (free will), a relationship that could have worked will unravel.

If the spirit guides say three times that it's over, then I'll assume there's either some kind of abuse going on or that the couple should have gone their separate ways years earlier.

SECOND CHANCES

Rebecca met Rick at college. They were everyone's idea of the perfect couple. "My family adored him," she said. "I did too. He embodied everything I admired about strong men. He was athletic, funny, and super-smart. We were going to get married. Then he cheated on me with my girlfriend."

Even though Rick was a soulmate, and being together was the result of a mutual agreement, Rebecca broke off the engagement. After graduation they moved to opposite sides of the country.

Fast forward twenty-five years and Rebecca, who is recently divorced, gets a message through social media from Rick. Now he's divorced, too, and living just a few towns away. He's wondering (not simply out of curiosity) what she's up to these days.

When two souls with a romantic agreement fail to complete their mission together, it can leave one or both with a sense of unfinished business. Souls often pine for the love they lost.

Rebecca had always wondered, "What if..." A part of her was curious to meet up with Rick and fantasized about rekindling the relationship. On the other hand, she'd been deeply hurt by his infidelity and wasn't entirely sure if seeing him again was such a good idea. She decided to check things out with me. The spirit guides were quick to remind her that she has total free will. If she chose to rekindle things, it was up to her. There was no wrong or right.

What Rebecca's soul wanted to avoid was a repetition of events. It put her on a kind of hair trigger when it came to disloyalty. The underlying cause was a past-life fear of Betrayal, the result of abandonment by a lover in Italy almost a century ago.

The spirit guides advised her that if she chose to see Rick again, she should move slowly. "Take your time. It's not a race," they stressed. She ended up having several dates with him. It was on the third one that he blew it with her. At 1:00 a.m. in her apartment, he received a text. Rebecca never found out who it was from, or what it said, but the way Rick cupped his hand around the phone, shielding it from her, was all it took to trigger her fear.

Rebecca used her free will to end things that night and since then has met a new guy who she trusts completely. The feeling of there being unfinished business with her ex has completely disappeared.

A lot of souls with broken agreements are now reuniting through social media. When they do, their souls will have the choice to renew the agreements or call it null and void. But, without calling me, or another psychic, how do you know if the agreement is still in place?

If you have an agreement that's still viable, even after decades apart, your spirit guides will conspire to make things happen. The biggest sign is actually very simple to identify. It's called the path of least resistance. If one of the pair has a portable skill, for example, and is willing to relocate, or if both feel there's nothing getting in the way of moving forward, then this should be regarded as a sign that the relationship is encouraged.

Conversely, if like my client Judy you meet someone you used to know, but now they have a drinking problem and anger issues, then that should be something to make you stop and consider where you're going. And if you have huge geographical or emotional mountains to climb, then pay attention. Long distance relationships can, and often do, work. But if the hurdles are almost insurmountable, and getting together is a monumental struggle, it's important to question whether the results are worth the effort.

If the agreement between two souls is null and void, there will be obstacles everywhere. Sometimes the chemistry is no longer there. You might just get a gut feeling—literally discomfort in your tummy—that tells you your paths are not aligned. Very often, too, your friends will notice something is amiss.

Of course, paying attention to signs from the universe isn't just something you want to do when an old flame drops you a line. It applies to every decision you make. The more you can check in with your feelings, the easier it becomes to make decisions that are in your best interest. Your emotions, it's important to remember, are the voice of your soul.

Your life plan is your route map, but you have virtually unlimited free will. Understanding your destiny allows you to navigate your path with confidence, knowing what's consistent with your soul's plan.

Remember, *your destiny is not some intangible, distant goal that you might, if you're lucky, discover sometime before you die. As long as it's consistent with your life plan, your destiny is what you're doing right now.* I can't emphasize this enough.

EXERCISE: TRUSTING YOUR INTUITION

The following exercise is designed to help you learn to trust your ability to make decisions by recognizing how often you've made choices as a result of following your intuition.

1. List three decisions you've made that you knew were in your highest interest, even when others might have disagreed.
2. List three times you ignored your intuition and made a decision because other people persuaded you to.

This is an exercise worth spending time on. You might notice that your intuition is a lot stronger than you thought. Keeping a journal listing your gut feelings about people and events in your life can be useful. Looking back and seeing how often you were right is a powerful way to validate your intuition.

When you learn to use your free will to follow your destiny, everything gets a little easier. It doesn't mean you'll suddenly win the lottery or marry a movie star, but you'll notice you don't have quite the same struggles as before. When people talk about going with the flow, what they really mean is that they're making decisions consistent with their life plan.

Perhaps the most important decision your soul makes, however, is not during this incarnation. As part of your life plan, your soul chose your personality. It was all part of the lengthy preparation it underwent on the Astral Plane before you were born. Your soul wanted to ensure that your personality would match your destiny. It was a choice, as you'll see, that was not made lightly.

4

SCALING MT. EVEREST IN FLIP FLOPS

CHOOSING AN APPROPRIATE
PERSONALITY FOR THE JOURNEY

*O*ne of the most profound statements I've heard from my spirit guides is also one of the simplest: "Who you are is why you're here." They mean that understanding your life's purpose begins with knowing your true personality—the one your soul chose before you were born.

Every soul comes into this world with a complete personality. And that shouldn't come as a total surprise. As I like to say, anyone who thinks babies are born as blank slates has clearly never met one.

Your personality is based on ten soul types, each one comprised of specific traits and behaviors developed over many lifetimes. Soul types not only define your true personality but, once you discover what they are, help you better understand what you're here on earth to do. As the spirit guides put it, "Soul types are a way to differentiate between traits that are expressions of fear and traits that express the essence of who you are."

With only ten soul types, what accounts for the apparent diversity of characteristics we see in human beings? The answer is that your soul type is simply the core of who you are. Add to that a primary influence of one of the other nine, and several secondary influences, and suddenly you have almost limitless variations.

Yet, despite there being thousands of combinations available, what makes it easy to identify who you truly are is that no matter how complex it might seem, there are always just ten soul types.

I introduced the concept of soul types in my book, *The Instruction*. If you've read it, I hope you'll find new insights here. And if you're new to the subject, I hope this will help you to gain a deeper understanding of yourself and others. Let's begin by looking at those soul types and their defining characteristic, both positive and negative.

THE TEN SOUL TYPES

- **Helper Types** are fulfilled by being of service to others or to the community. They are practical and grounded, and comfortable with mundane or repetitive tasks. On the downside, they can lack drive or ambition.
- **Caregiver Types** are nurturing, empathic, and drawn to careers like counseling and healing, where they can apply their compassion and understanding. Unfortunately, their tendency to put others ahead of themselves can cause them to neglect their own needs.
- **Educator Types** want to teach, inform, or impart knowledge in some way. They are eloquent, patient, and need students of some kind. They can slip easily into being long-winded.
- **Thinker Types** are intellectually centered, drawn to academia, books, and classes, and like to travel. Their attention to detail helps them excel in work in areas like law, programming, and science. Almost every

Thinker struggles with a tendency to be over-analytical.

- **Creator Types** are highly sensitive, imaginative and, as the name suggests, creative. They require the freedom to make their own decisions. They risk being ungrounded or unworldly.
- **Performer Types** are outgoing, communicative, and playful. They are drawn to the stage, dance, music, and generally being in the spotlight. A sense of humor helps temper a tendency to be pretentious or dramatic.
- **Hunter Types** are active, goal-oriented, and very much in their bodies. They work well in teams, and like sports, either as a participant or a spectator. Their single-mindedness can make them inflexible or resistant to change.
- **Leader Types** are comfortable taking charge or asserting authority. They are often charismatic, are at home in the outdoors, and need exercise to feel complete. Their decisive nature can slip easily into intransigence.
- **Spiritualist Types** seek meaning and want to see a better world while working on their own self-development. They're drawn to alternative and traditional healing. All Spiritualists risk becoming obsessive in their quest for improvement in themselves or others.
- **Transformer Types** are rare but share several characteristics. They are inspirational and charismatic, inspire social change, and always develop a passionate following. Their idealism and fearlessness can make them unworldly and disinterested in their personal safety.

Again, who you are is inseparable from why you're here. You wouldn't wear flip flops to climb Everest, just as you wouldn't choose the Leader soul type as part of your personality if you were never going to have anyone to lead. You choose your soul type and influences carefully, aware of the lessons and major life experiences your soul wants to explore in any particular incarnation.

Every time you plan a new incarnation, you select an appropriate soul type and influences. In one life, you might feel being a Creator with a Thinker influence will suit you best. In the next, you might choose to be an Educator type with a Hunter influence. As your soul ages, however, it develops favorites, and may cycle between two or three particular combinations.

LEADING THE WAY

Emily is a force to be reckoned with. As a 13-year old Leader type, she has traveled internationally to attend summer schools and plans to eventually work on eradicating malaria. I told her mother, my client, that I imagined she'd have seen signs of her daughter's Leader influence at a very young age.

"Definitely!" her mother said, "She potty-trained herself at 18 months, and because of her, all the other pre-school kids followed her lead. They were all potty-trained before the age of two."

Knowing your soul type and influences leads to a more fulfilling and purposeful life. Self-knowledge is the key to self-empowerment. The better you know yourself, the easier it is to make choices that enhance your journey through this life. Remember, "who you are is why you're here."

So, how did you learn to be who you are? Since you've been incarnating and reincarnating for millennia, it helps to look back at the past to the experiences that have shaped your personality.

From the late Stone Age until modern times, you've been working on developing the traits and behaviors associated with each soul type. And your search for growth and knowledge has continually pushed the tribe to expand its horizons. Which is why the world is ever-changing.

Yet, no matter where you look back to in history, you'll see the same ten soul types at work. They show up in all cultures and in every period of human development.

In the next section, we'll examine life in the Stone Age and London in the 1600s to show how your soul types gradually developed to make you the person you are now.

THE ORIGIN OF SOUL TYPES

We humans first developed identifiable soul types about 55,000 years ago. Back then, the tribe, though primitive, was a place in which everyone had a clear purpose.

In a simpler society, your soul type was easily identified. You knew your purpose, and others knew it, too. Tribal elders didn't waste time pushing physically energetic Hunters to take care of the children, or sticking spears in the hands of nurturing Caregivers and sending them out to track down dinner.

There was respect, too, for each other's individuality. Grounded Leader types didn't look down their noses at Creators because of their sensitivity, and Thinkers didn't judge Helpers as lesser because they were not as intellectually centered.

As an old soul, your journey on the Physical Plane began something like 6,000 years ago. In the Neolithic era, tribal life had changed quite a bit from the time we humans first started developing our soul types. You would have grown up using technology like stone axes, ploughs, and millstones that had not existed 50,000 years earlier.

Your first few incarnations as a hunter-gatherer, or even an early farmer, would have allowed your ethereal self to simply get used to being in a body. Your lessons would not have extended much beyond those related to staying alive. However, even the simplest of lives allowed you to try out different soul types.

Though not consciously, we recognized that every person in the tribe made a valuable contribution. We relied on the Hunter types to protect us and, as the name suggests, to hunt. We looked to Leader types to guide the tribe to new places when food became scarce. We needed Caregiver soul types to take care of the sick and dying.

By the 17th Century, however, we'd started to lose a sense of the important role each of us played in the smooth running of the community. Active Hunter types often atrophied behind desks in actuarial offices, and sensitive Creator types ended up wielding bows and arrows on far-flung battlefields. Instead of gravitating toward careers best suited to us, we often had others choose them for us.

The life you planned wouldn't always work out. Yet, in the main, most incarnations were successful, and the soul type and influences you chose for each journey would be the ones you'd end up using. In the 21st Century, however, fewer of us than ever are recognized for the innate abilities that come with our Soul types. (I don't imagine anyone has ever acknowledged the thousands of years of effort that have gone into you becoming the person you are now.)

Your soul type is the core of who you are. It gives you the behavior and traits that determine your life purpose. And it's worth stressing that your day job is not necessarily your life purpose. It can be, of course. And if you look back at your past lives, it's often the day job, or the way you spent the larger part of your days, that helped you develop the characteristics you manifest in this incarnation. Let's look at all ten soul types and the kind of experiences that have helped you learn to be you.

THE HELPER TYPE

For obvious reasons, your lack of worldly experience would not have made you a wise and decisive leader in your first life. That's why you and every other soul started out on the Physical Plane as a Helper type—a follower, not a leader. In the Stone Age, you'd have carried water, skinned carcasses, built homes, and kept the fire going. Everything you did was for common good. All souls learn from one another. As a Helper type, you came out of the womb preprogramed to learn from other Helpers.

London in the 17th Century was an overcrowded, smoky, smelly, yet vibrant and complex city. The population grew from around 250,000 in 1600, to over 600,000 by the end of the century.

Your lives as a Helper type in the Stone Age, keeping daily life in the tribe ticking over, taking care of the day-to-day business of life, eventually morphed into the butcher, baker, and candlestick-maker of Tudor England.

If you chose to be a Helper type at that time, there would have been plenty of ways to be of service to the community. You might have enjoyed exploring such crafts as brewing, baking, carpentry, or masonry. You could well have added to the funky atmosphere of the place with some of the more unpleasant jobs, like tanning hides, butchering animals, or catching rats. (Someone has to do it, and Helpers are the ones least likely to turn up their noses at such work.)

If you're a Helper type in this life, you'll be fulfilled being of service to others. You'll be practical, and you'll know how to use the tools of your trade (whether it's a screwdriver, a cash register, a laptop, or a steering wheel). You may not be overly ambitious, and that's okay. You're not here to change the world, but to help it run more smoothly.

THE CAREGIVER TYPE

As a Caregiver type in the Stone Age tribe, you were involved in caring for children, tending animals, taking care of the sick, and helping the dying prepare to cross over to the Astral Plane. It's through being a Caregiver more than any other soul type that we develop empathy. Empathy is the ability to put yourself in another's place, and also, as the spirit guides put it, "to pick up on non-verbal emotional signals."

Once you got to the 1600s, you continued building your empathy through activities like delivering babies, raising children, and all kinds of nursing, formal and informal. With plague, smallpox, and typhoid amongst the many diseases to afflict Londoners, you'd have had ample opportunity to develop the nurturing and compassionate qualities associated with Caregivers.

THE NEED TO NURTURE

I was talking to a client about her soul types. "You're a Caregiver type," I said.

"I read *The Instruction*," she said, "And that was the soul type that most resonated with me."

"Many of my Caregiver clients are hospice workers." I added.

She said, "I'm training to be a hospice nurse."

Less than 48-hours later, I was reading another client who turned out to be a Caregiver type. I said, "I don't encounter a lot of full-blown Caregivers in my work [It's more usually an influence], but you're one. Funnily enough, I was just talking to a Caregiver a couple of days ago. She's training to be a hospice worker. What do you do?"

He said, "I'm training to be a hospice nurse."

You'll know you're a Caregiver type by the deep sense of purpose you get from nurturing and taking care of others. You probably notice your tendency to put their needs ahead of your own, and that's a weakness you share with most other Caregivers. Self care doesn't come easily to such giving souls, and is something you'll always have to work on.

In your history as a Caregiver, you've had many lifetimes when you were there at the beginning of life (the midwife) and at the end (the death doula or hospice worker). You'll intuitively get what a toddler is trying to tell you, and your animal karma will be exceptional: they'll love you as much as you love them. And that's why you'll be drawn to activities that allow you to care for others, human and animal.

THE EDUCATOR TYPE

As an Educator type in the Stone Age, you would have put everything you learned into action as you shaped young minds and taught others what you knew. In this role, you might have been the wise woman, guiding young women through puberty, or the herbalist teaching others how to use flowers, barks and seeds as medicine.

In Elizabethan England, you'd have had plenty of schools and places of education to be a teacher and explore the Educator type in you. You could have been a mentor to a young apprentice or used your desire to impart knowledge to the world through a newspaper.

You'll recognize the Educator type in you by the seriousness with which you take getting your point across. Long before anyone else has even thought about solving a problem, you've already seen the best way forward and, dammit, you need to make sure they understand that your way is the best!

Whether you're teaching Ninth Grade calculus, briefing a bomber crew, or reminding your children to stay clear of strangers, you have to make sure everyone gets it. "Now, repeat back what I just told you..."

Few Educator types value brevity over comprehension, and in a stuffy conference room, they're the ones who infuriate their more impatient colleagues with phrases like, "Let's just go over it one last time..."

THE THINKER TYPE

You developed your intellect from lives as a Thinker type. In the Stone Age, without books to learn from, your school was the world around you. You learned how tools were made, how to judge the best time to sow and reap crops, and how to make sense of the sun, the moon, and the stars. You were the tribal intellectual and archivist.

In the 17th Century, Thinker types led the way during a time when science and technology began taking a leap forward. You would have expanded your innate curiosity and attention to detail through being a civil servant, an academic, an explorer, a lawyer, a clockmaker or, perhaps, a printer or publisher.

If you're reading this, it's highly likely you have the Thinker type in the mix somewhere. You'll know it's your soul type if you constantly analyze and question everything and regard the left-hemisphere of your brain as home. Thinker types often sit quietly during my workshops, scribbling furiously with such attention to detail you'd think they were court stenographers.

There's nothing wrong with that—it's just their way of processing.

The downside of this reliance on the rational mind is the curse of the Thinker—a tendency to over analyze to a point of paralysis.

THE CREATOR TYPE

Back in prehistoric times, you explored what it meant to be a Creator type in lots of, well, creative ways. You would have applied your innate creativity to making jewelry, clothing, and pottery. Your imagination might have been responsible for making food more interesting. In fact, whatever you turned your hand to became something more than just functional. Creators added decoration to elevate practical everyday objects into pieces of art.

Moving forward a few thousand years, and a city like London was the perfect place for Creators to thrive. You might have become a portrait painter, or been involved in making ceramic pipes for the tobacco that Sir Walter Raleigh had recently introduced to England from the New World.

Opportunities to express creativity were everywhere. Someone had to make ladies' fans, or the playing cards that had become the latest fad. And it was Creator types who would design and create objects in glass, ceramics, silver, and gold for those who could afford them.

All Creator types need the freedom to make their own decisions. Many are self-employed, and most would like to be. You'll know you're one if you're used to hearing yourself described as sensitive (usually along with the prefix "overly.") But it's the Creator sensitivity that allows you tap easily into past lives, and even the Astral Plane, for inspiration.

Creators are emotional creatures and often converse in superlatives: "It's the best restaurant in Manhattan, and their desserts are works of art." They can be somewhat ungrounded. Yet it's that Creator otherworldliness that allows them such an easy connection to the other side.

―――――――

RESONANCES FROM THE PAST

Your sense of smell has the ability to instantly connect you with your past, both in this and other lives. At the beginning of Cecilia's first session with me, I asked my spirit guides for anything they wanted to tell me about her.

They said, "She was a portrait painter in a past life. It gave her a strong sense of purpose. And she'll resonate with the smell of oil paint."

"Are you an artist?" I asked.

Cecilia laughed. She said, "I started oil painting when I was 13. My Twitter bio says 'Passionate about B2B marketing. Love the smell of oil paints. Hoping to make a positive impact.'"

The next time we spoke, Cecilia said, "Our conversation helped to validate many things I'd been thinking about for a long time. Now I'm getting ready to quit my job at Google and join a non-profit organization that focuses on emotional intelligence and mindfulness. Knowing my purpose makes me realize it's the right next step to take."

―――――――

THE PERFORMER TYPE

As a Performer type, you learned to dance, sing, and tell the story of the hunt through mime. Performer types can be a lot more emotionally centered than most. Their emotions are often huge and their need for approval even larger. Stone Age Hunter and Leader types didn't stop in the middle of tracking a deer to deal with hurt feelings and offer group hugs. But Performers when they got together would.

With a fashionable venue like Shakespeare's Globe Theater to hang out in, Performer types in the 17th Century never had it so good. As a Performer then, you could also have expressed yourself through music or dance. But there was one unexpected place where Performer types thrived: the inn. Since every Performer type seeks an audience, being a bartender was the perfect occupation. Pubs made a perfect stage and came with a ready-made audience.

Most Performers are comfortable in the spotlight, and that's where they're meant to be. If you're a Performer in the 21st Century, you'll have certain traits that stand out.

The first is a sense of humor. A quick wit is something shared by Performers worldwide.

The second is that you'll be what might be called a "people person." You should feel at ease around others and have some level of natural charm or even charisma.

The third is a facility with language. Sometimes this is the ability to pick up foreign languages but can also be a talent for mimicry.

If your soul decided you should travel through this life as a Performer, it's because it expects you to find an audience at some point. You might be drawn to the stage as you were in Shakespeare's day. Or you may end up in a job that requires you to present in front of groups or be part of a sales team.

If a Performer doesn't get the recognition they require, they'll sometimes act out till they get it. A child will throw a tantrum, or Great Aunt Maisie will use her chronic ailments to get attention. Many martyrs are Performers who didn't get enough attention when they were children.

THE HUNTER TYPE

The rough and tumble world of Stone Age humans was the perfect environment for a Hunter type to thrive. It allowed you to stretch yourself physically and, since your function was to ensure the survival of the tribe, you hunted, fished, and guarded against attacks from wild animals and belligerent enemies.

As a Hunter type in 1600's England, your purview—the safety and wellbeing of the tribe—was the same as it had always been. You would have guarded the city gates, piloted vessels on the River Thames, or ridden horses and stagecoaches.

And when the Great Fire of London broke out in 1666, you and your fellow firefighters would have been the ones blowing up and demolishing houses to prevent the flames from spreading.

Hunter types are here to be active. They work well individually and together, and make perfect loyal lieutenants to their Leader type generals. The need to get things done goes back to the time of the tribe. They had one job to do: ensure the survival of all.

If you're a Hunter type, this single-minded approach to your work will make you task-oriented and tenacious. You just need to know what's wanted, and when, and you'll make it happen.

Also, if you're a Hunter type, you might be reading this in the gym. Exercise is as essential to your wellbeing as oxygen. As a Hunter, you should love hiking, biking, walking, skiing, surfing, swimming, running and generally raising a sweat.

It all goes back to your active purpose in the tribe. Exercise allows a Hunter type to unite mind, body, and spirit.

Hunter types almost always share a common trait. They can be incredibly inflexible. They have a plan, it worked before, and now they're going to see it through, even if it doesn't seem to be working.

The world is full of Hunters bashing their heads against the proverbial brick wall. Hunters are usually economic with their words, and reserved when it comes to expressing their emotions.

THE LEADER TYPE

Behind all great Hunter types is a Leader type making the big decisions. As a Leader in the Neolithic period, your innate common sense or wisdom, and comfort making decisions would have caused you to stand out. Every other soul type would have known to defer to you.

In the 17th Century, at a time when hierarchies were in every walk of life, you would have explored being a Leader in a professional guild, the church, the burgeoning bureaucracy, or the military. You'd have learned to use authority (hopefully wisely) through being a judge, a bishop, a general, or a boss of some sort.

If you're a Leader type now, you'll need people to lead. You might be a bandleader, a project manager, a team leader, an airline pilot, or a motivational speaker, and you should have noticed by now that people will put you in a position of authority without you even asking. After many lifetimes spent outdoors, nature should be a place in which you feel comfortable. And having been a person of action, you should enjoy playing and watching sports or working out.

I'M STARTING TO LOSE MY PATIENCE HERE!

For some souls, having to endure childhood can lead to frustration. A few years ago, I told my client, John, that his four-year old son, Bobby, was a Leader type. "Is he bossy?" I asked.

"Oh yeah," John said, "He marches around the house

issuing orders to everyone. And he doesn't like being told what to do.

The other morning, he asked me for his sippy cup. I said, 'We talked about this last night. You've not been eating your breakfast, so you're not getting a sippy cup until afterwards.'

A few minutes later, I heard him upstairs, asking his mom the same questions. She told him what I just had. The next thing, he walks straight up to me and says, 'Dad...you're pissing me off. Give me my sippy cup!'"

It can be infuriating being a Leader when others tell you what to do. Which leads us to a weakness all Leaders will encounter: intransigence. Once a Leader makes a decision, it's made. They'll often ignore the opinions of others, even when they're right.

THE SPIRITUALIST TYPE

Since every tribe needed someone to act as a bridge between this world and the next, your earliest lives as a Spiritualist type would have been as a priest or shaman. But you also had another function, and that was to be a healer.

Though you may question the credentials of a physician who bleeds patients, you've been there. Your lives as a Spiritualist type in the 1600s were ones with greater than ever potential for learning. You might have studied with William Harvey who, in 1628, published his radical theory that blood circulated the body.

Of course, you might just as easily have bought into the theory that all disease is an imbalance in humors, cured by bleeding and other even more drastic treatments. As an old-soul Spiritualist, however, your intentions will generally have been the best, and you'll have played an important part in the history of medicine.

Most of my clients are Spiritualist types. They're looking for meaning through being of some kind of higher service. That's why I have more clients who are physicians than any other single occupation, followed by healers of all kinds, from acupuncturists to therapists.

Being a Spiritualist type means doing something bigger than yourself. Your soul aims to leave this world a better place than it was when it entered.

There is, however, a small flaw shared by many Spiritualists. It's the inability to let go when you need to. You might meet some frustrating resistance when you're trying to help someone. Remember, they have to want whatever it is you offer more than you do.

THE TRANSFORMER TYPE

Though you cycled through the various soul types with regularity, there was one you might never have had the opportunity to experience: the Transformer.

Such a soul is rare and is someone with a combination of the Spiritualist and Leader types who is also on their last life. In Stone Age times, a Transformer might have led a slave's revolt, or played a significant part in overthrowing a corrupt leader.

A Transformer in Elizabethan times, with their Spiritualist/Transformer soul-type combination would have stood out from the crowd.

The upside is that they would have inevitably made a significant difference in many peoples' lives.

The downside is that they would have been the target of younger souls who tend to like things just as they are. They might well have been locked up in the Tower of London to curb their revolutionary zeal, or ended up dangling from a noose.

It's never safe to be a Transformer, but the urge to create a better world usually causes such idealistic old souls to neglect their personal safety for the higher good of humanity.

The desire for a higher purpose is taken to an even higher level in Transformers who are, after all, not just Leaders, but Spiritualists, too. Nelson Mandela and John Lennon were both here to lead, inspire, and initiate change.

Technically speaking (and I'm being really pedantic here), they were Quasi-Transformers. They were very old souls, and they had the required Spiritualist/Leader combination in their soul types, but neither was on his last life. Nevertheless, we can consider them to be Transformers.

Are you a Transformer? You'll have a strong sense of fairness, a remarkable lack of fear concerning your own personal safety, and you'll attract devoted followers. Being close to the end of all your lives on the Physical Plane, you're looking to go out with a bang.

And, like Gandhi, Martin Luther King Jr., and every other Transformer, you'll strike fear into the hearts of the young-soul establishment. It's highly likely the Feds will have a file on you.

EMBRACE YOURSELF

Your soul type and influences make you who you are, and they didn't spring out of nowhere. You've spent thousands of years learning to be you.

I encourage you to embrace the person you truly are, and have fun exploring activities and interests that are consistent with your true personality.

Knowing who you are brings you closer to knowing why you're here. So be yourself, and fly your soul-type flag with pride!

And don't forget to support others in being who they truly are. They've spent thousands of years learning to be who they are too.

EXERCISE: FIND YOUR SOUL TYPE

Take a few moments to ground and open yourself, then read through the following traits associated with each soul type. Choose the one that resonates most strongly with you. Don't sweat it—just use your intuition.

Once you feel comfortable with your top choice, choose a primary influence from one of the other nine. And once you've got that, see which of the others speak to you. Those are your secondary influences.

You can take the Soul Type Quiz on my website (ainsliemacleod.com) to see how closely your results align.

The Ten Soul Types:

- **Helper:** Of Service, Practical, Passive
- **Caregiver:** Nurturing, Empathic, Prone to Self-Neglect
- **Educator:** Informative, Eloquent, Verbose
- **Thinker:** Rational, Curious, Over-Analytical
- **Creator:** Sensitive, Creative, Ungrounded
- **Performer:** Communicative, Playful, Pretentious
- **Hunter:** Physical, Task-Oriented, Inflexible
- **Leader:** Charismatic, Active, Intransigent
- **Spiritualist:** Compassionate, Spiritual/Religious, Obsessive
- **Transformer:** Inspirational, Motivational, Unworldly

As an old soul, you're driven to manifest who you are, and you can never truly know who you are without understanding the origins of your personality. That awareness helps you find ways to best express the person you truly are. And that leads to living a far happier and more spiritually fulfilling life.

Your past lives are responsible for the traits and behaviors that shape your personality. But that's only part of the story. Your past lives were not always happy or fulfilling, and things didn't always work out as planned.

Throughout the thousands of years in which you've been exploring the human world, you've suffered everything from devastating loss to heart-wrenching abandonment.

All the hurts and disappointments you've endured have shaped who you are, which is why it's essential to understand the way traumatic events from prior incarnations interfere with your ability to fully live the life your soul intended during this phase of the voyage. And why it's important to learn how to overcome that interference.

II

OBSTACLES IN YOUR PATH

5

WHY PAST LIVES MATTER

YOU CAN'T TELL WHERE YOU'RE GOING IF YOU DON'T KNOW WHERE YOU'VE BEEN

*E*very day, I become increasingly convinced that there is absolutely nothing we experience in this life that isn't related to our many (and often traumatic) past lives. I firmly maintain that you can never fully know who you *are* if you don't know who you *were.* And you can't tell where you're *going* if you don't know where you've *been.*

There's a common assumption that we don't remember our past lives. I argue that we do, but we just don't always do it consciously. Past-life memories not only show up in the talents and skills we possess now, they also show up as limiting beliefs, fears, phobias, and the physical ailments I call Achilles body parts. It's not that we don't remember our past lives. We just don't know what to look for.

When an event in this life triggers a traumatic past-life memory, your soul starts to over-react. Irrationally, it thinks that whatever awful thing took place in the past is about to happen again.

Would you rather die than give a speech? Maybe not, but for many people, the mere idea of getting up in front of an audience is enough to trigger a butt-clenching fear response. You probably won't die, but your soul isn't so sure. It remembers how judgment once led to death in another lifetime, and that triggers a fight-or-flight reaction in this one.

If you were once sentenced to death in a court of law, your soul might equate your audience with the magistrates whose judgment sealed your fate. The moment the fear is triggered, mind, body, and spirit go into a tailspin. Your voice shakes nervously, and your legs feel like they're about to give way beneath you. It's hard to think rationally when your soul is freaking out. You start to panic and forget what you were going to say. (It's like trying to focus on a crossword puzzle with a smoke alarm shrieking above your head.)

Although we associate phobias with panic attacks, in spirit guide parlance, a phobia is simply a death-related fear. But when your soul is triggered by a reminder of death, perhaps a thousand years ago, its response can cause a panic attack in a nanosecond.

The intensity of your reaction to a past-life trigger can take you (and others) by surprise. A client who once went down with a ship was led out of the theater in tears during the movie Titanic.

Another, who'd been previously restrained and tortured in a Russian prison, went into a full-blown panic attack when, as a child, she got tangled in the bed sheets during a sleepover at her friend's house. "I could have rolled out," she told me, "But I was paralyzed by fear. Even now I remember how intense it felt."

PHOBIC REACTIONS

Before I healed my fear of public speaking (with the help of my spirit guides), my fight-or-flight reaction to the mere idea of public speaking threatened to give me a heart attack.

One time, my friend Chris (who shared the same fear)

asked me, "Would you rather lose a finger than give a speech?"

"Which finger," I asked.

"The little one," he said.

"How much? The whole finger, or just part of it?"

As crazy as this conversation may sound, we earnestly agreed that losing an entire pinky was a reasonable alternative to speaking in public!

Soon after that conversation, I healed the fear by finding its past-life source, and was perfectly comfortable giving a speech at Chris's wedding. And if you question the veracity of this story, I'd be happy and somewhat relieved to be able to pinky swear that it's true.

When you trigger a past-life memory, something that was never an issue before is suddenly front and center. The breakup of a relationship might bring up past-life fears of Betrayal (causing mistrust), Rejection (causing feelings of abandonment), or Intimacy (causing you to swear you'll be a lot more careful before opening your heart to someone in the future).

Irrational is a word we often use to describe fears and negative beliefs that seem to have no logical reason for existing. But once you realize that the cause lies in events from previous incarnations, however weird it may seem, it makes much more sense.

Since you've reincarnated scores of times by now, it's inevitable that you'll carry reminders of your soul's checkered past with you into this life.

Do you have issues with low self-esteem? Do you procrastinate? Are you a perfectionist? Do you struggle with unexplained anxiety? Do you feel like an outsider who never really fits in?

These symptoms (and many more) are the result of events that may have occurred lifetimes ago. And though you might point the finger at your uncaring mother, or put your problems down to a troubled childhood, what happened to you in this life was a trigger, not the cause.

This is why two people react very differently to the same traumatic event in this life. One might see what happened as being all about betrayal, while the other might see it as rejection.

A SHORT GLOSSARY

When I discuss past lives, I use certain specific terms. This short glossary should help explain what each one means.

Cause: Let's say, for example, you were accused of theft and sentenced to death two hundred years ago.

Fear: Though your soul is essentially fearless, it carries the memory of the past-life trauma, in this case, Judgment.

Resonance: A resonance in this life would be anxiety around public speaking, a fear of sitting tests, stage fright, or a heightened concern about what others say or think of you. Anything that makes you feel judged.

Block: If your fear interferes with your life, it's a block. It might be that you're unable to get promoted because you can't give presentations.

Trigger: Being asked to give a presentation to 200 people causes the fear to be triggered and brought into the mind or body.

A block is the issue you want to overcome. If you're stuck in a job you hate, that's the block. The resonance might be low self-esteem that makes you feel you're not worthy of anything better. A trigger for the feelings of low self-esteem might be criticism from your boss.

A past-life resonance like procrastination stems from failure or loss in another incarnation. The block might be that you're afraid to start your own business or follow through with certain activities because you don't believe things will work out.

You'll see it in children who give up really easily saying, "I'll never be able to do it!" Sadly, they're often the ones who grow up to become expert procrastinators.

Loneliness or the feeling of being an outsider is a resonance from a life of abandonment, and the block is a tendency to isolate or to push relationships away.

A trigger doesn't have to be huge to take your soul back to the original event, and catapult the emotions created centuries ago into the present.

Crossing a bridge might instantly trigger a fear of heights. But not all triggers are quite as obvious or dramatic.

A more low-level reminder, like your parents' disinterest in you, might act as a constant trigger for your past-life fear of Inferiority, and cause you to settle for second best in relationships or feel like an imposter at work.

The daughter of one of my clients has a past-life fear that's triggered instantly by the sight of a needle. She has to be sedated before she can have a shot, and she's been like this since she was just a few months old.

The moment her skin was first punctured, her soul recalled the terrifying moment a cobra once sank its fangs into her. In that past life, it had killed her. In this, just the memory is enough to cause her to pass out.

Most past-life fears lie dormant until someone or something acts as a trigger. And for a very sensitive old soul, the memory can be triggered by an event that seems relatively insignificant.

LOST IN TRANSLATION

For some of my clients, English is not their first language. One is an Indian woman who learned English in the U.K. She'd died in a cramped prison cell in a previous lifetime, and that's the kind of thing that invariably results in a fear of enclosed spaces.

I asked her, "Are you afraid of elevators?"

She thought about it for a few seconds, and replied, "No, but I am terrified of lifts!" (And in the unlikely event you don't know, a lift is what we Brits call an elevator.)

ONE LONG LIFE

Your soul has a fundamental problem. You might be on life 120, but your soul is not. Your physical body may return to dust on the completion of each incarnation, but your soul keeps on going.

From your soul's perspective, this is life number one. It's been conscious throughout all your incarnations, and what happened 5,000-years ago is still fresh in its memory.

Think of it this way: If a dog bit you when you were a child in this life, you might get anxious around dogs now. In the same way, your soul worries that whatever happened before, even a thousand years ago, is going to happen again.

You'd think your soul would have all the answers, but it doesn't. Even after endlessly repeating the cycle of life and death, it has to be reminded that what happened in the past was in another lifetime—that "that was then, and this is now"—which is the key to healing.

ESCAPING HELPLESSNESS

I told my client, Jane, how she'd drowned during World War II in particularly frightening circumstances. She was a young man, a sailor, whose ship was attacked. An explosion caused the ship to lurch, and he was thrown off the stern into the ocean.

He ended up underwater, tossed around like a rag doll, helpless to avoid being drawn into the ship's propeller. Looking up, he saw the sea on fire; looking down, he saw only darkness.

Jane had always felt unable to escape this place of helplessness. She was married to an abusive man, and though she'd left him three times before, she'd always gone back out of fear. "I've always had an extreme feeling of being trapped in my life circumstance," she said.

She also had vertigo, a direct resonance from being thrown around in the turbulent water during that traumatic past life. Significantly, in this life, she had a terrible fear of propellers, and would warn her children obsessively about how dangerous they could be when they were at the beach.

Jane got in touch after the session to tell me how things had changed. "Doctors couldn't ever find a cause for my vertigo," she said. They were suggesting surgery to fix it, even though they didn't know why it was happening.

"Every night following the session, however, I would lie down and turn to my right (which was always when the vertigo hit). As I would spin and spin, I reminded my soul that I was on solid ground, that I was no longer being tossed around under the water.

"Exactly one week to the day from our call, the vertigo ceased. I can now lay down to sleep! I can turn my head any which way I want!"

And there was more. "Just over one month from our session, I finally left my husband of 17 years for good! I used to say, 'I feel like I'll die either way, whether I leave him or stay.' But now my kids are thriving and I'm happy, and I don't feel as if I'm going to die anymore. I am beyond excited to see what is next for me!"

NIGHT AS A TIME OF FEAR

Do you struggle with insomnia? Do you lay awake until it's light outside? Do you jump at every bump and creak, convinced someone's in the house?

At an event in San Francisco, I asked participants if they woke up at a certain time during the night. The response was amazing. They shouted out specific times like 4:17 or 2:34. And when I observed that many people get their best sleep just as the sun starts coming up, there were many nods of recognition.

If, in a past life, you were attacked and killed during the hours of darkness, then in this life, your soul will fear dropping its guard. It will cause you to be on high alert when you should be resting. It might keep you awake so you can escape trouble. And if you wake up at a certain time every night, it may just be your soul making sure all is well. It worries that something will happen to once again cause your life plan to come to an abrupt and violent halt.

If you were killed in your home in another life, you'll check the doors and windows before bedtime. If you died at night away from home, then you may be reluctant to leave the house after dark.

HAIR TRIGGERS

Adina wasn't at all surprised when, in our first session together, I identified a huge past-life fear of what could happen at night and felt there had to have been a major trigger in this life.

"I was stalked for years," she said. "I never felt safe."

She told me how, one night, when she was in the house alone, she woke up hearing noises. She pulled out the .44 snubnose she kept under the pillow and crept into the hallway, dropping to one knee, the gun extended in front of her.

She crept through the house for twenty minutes before realizing the wind from an open window was causing a door to open and close.

What may seem like an over-reaction to one person makes total sense to another whose past-life fear of death has been brought to the surface by events in this life.

Steve, a young man from Los Angeles, had a life in Pennsylvania about a hundred years ago. Back then, he was a rather naïve boy who fell in love with an older woman.

When he caught the woman he worshipped in bed with another man, he lost his temper and attacked his rival. Unfortunately, he ended up getting badly beaten. And to make matters worse, the woman called the police. She claimed she'd never seen him before and accused him of being a burglar.

He spent years in a prison for a crime he hadn't committed. At night, when the lights went out, he suffered appalling physical and sexual abuse at the hands of older prisoners. Relief finally came when he died from TB after months in solitary confinement.

The memory of this lonely life was still alive and well. Aware that terrible things can happen during the hours of darkness, Steve's soul made sure he protected himself at all times. Since childhood, he had always slept with a nightlight. He would not only lock the door to his apartment at night, but also the one to his bedroom.

He suffered from chronic insomnia and would consider it a good night if he slept more than three hours. And he hated being touched. He had never been able to spend the night with his girlfriend. Needless to say, that wasn't helping his romantic life one bit.

When I spoke to Steve a few weeks after his session, everything had changed. The first sign of a shift came after he took a quick nap in the late afternoon. He woke up in the early evening to find he'd not only left the bedroom door open, but the front door, too. "Not a smart thing to do in L.A.," he remarked.

No longer afraid of what could happen during the hours of darkness, Steve's soul didn't have to keep him on high alert. He started sleeping through the night and, for the first time, was able to have his girlfriend spend the night with him. "I never thought it was possible," he told me.

Once Steve's soul was reminded that its fears were irrational, it recognized both that falling in love would not automatically result in rejection by his lover and that he'd no longer be vulnerable to attack when the lights went out.

SHARED FEARS

Sometimes family members will share the same fear. Having gone through the same traumatic experience in the past, they'll respond to the same triggers.

In 2013, I was teaching a workshop at Hollyhock, a retreat center on an island in British Columbia. One of the participants was a businesswoman whose tough exterior earned her the nickname "Krusty" from the group.

I told her about a past life she'd had in New York City in the earlier part of the 20th Century. She'd been a young boy, living in an apartment with his parents. One day, the phone rang and the boy picked it up. A voice on the other end said, "Your dad just died. Can I speak to your mother?"

The mother took the phone from her shocked son and got the same terse, matter-of-fact message: "You husband just died." The call was from a colleague of her husband, someone who clearly had a shocking lack of sensitivity.

At the start of World War II, the boy signed up for active service, and died soon after on a Pacific island, his legs cut off at the knees by machine gun fire.

When I told Denise what happened, she lost her Krusty-like composure. "I'm terrified of the phone," she said, as a tear ran down her cheek. "I can't answer it or even make a call."

I asked her about her knees. It was no surprise to learn that she suffered from chronic knee problems.

"Who was my mother in that life?" she asked. I looked across the room to where her daughter Maria was sitting. "You were the mother," I said.

By now, Maria was starting to tear up, too. "I have the same fear," she whispered. (By the way, this sort of thing is not uncommon, where participants in one of my live events turn out to have a shared past lifetime. It's a perfect example of how your spirit guides will lead you to connect with other souls to facilitate shared healing.)

Both mother and daughter suffered from a past-life fear of the unknown. Every time the phone rang, or they had to make a call, their souls went into a state of alarm.

Had the father lived, the son was destined to have become an actor, not a soldier, and would more than likely have survived the war. The mother would have seen her son live a happy and fulfilling life. Instead she lost her only child while he was still in his teens.

The death of the father was the catalyst that led to the son being taken off his life plan and his untimely death. The phone is the trigger that reminds both souls of the events that happened a lifetime ago.

A year later, Denise gave me an update. "My phone fear has

completely subsided," she said. "I can talk for an hour or more with friends and family without sweat running down my back. I can call a client now, where before I'd have had someone else do it, or I'd just have avoided it until the problem went away.

"My fear was like PTSD. The fight-or-flight mechanism would make my heart race, my body sweat, and I'd hyperventilate. I'd have to run to the bathroom, too."

Not only has Denise's phone fear gone, but her relationship with her daughter has undergone a huge shift, too. "When she was born, I really didn't like her," Denise said. "She screamed for ten months and we butted heads until she turned 15. We worked on forgiveness at the workshop and now, knowing she had once been my mother, our relationship has taken on a new meaning."

And her knees? "They didn't get better instantly," Denise said, "But now I hike, ski, and backpack without tensors or supports, and I feel comfortable going downhill. Before, I was always braced for disaster, like my knees would be 'cut out from under me.' I no longer need painkillers. Tomorrow I'm going on a 16-kilometer hike with 3,000 feet of elevation change each way."

There's one other interesting thing that happened at the retreat center. An hour after I told Denise about her past life, she was handing over her credit card in the gift shop. She turned to get her daughter's attention and—like Miranda who I talked about in Chapter Three—said, "Mom…"

TAKING RESPONSIBILITY

If you had a past life where you made a decision that caused your death or the death of others, then you might find it hard to choose between two dishes on a restaurant menu. (I joke that this is why surf and turf was invented.)

Some people whose souls carry this burden hate having to take responsibility for even the smallest decisions. One of my clients was so averse to taking responsibility that she'd never learned to drive. One young man I spoke to wouldn't buy a home because it required too much responsibility.

But others swing to the opposite end of the spectrum. Instead of avoiding responsibility, they take too much.

In a past life, my client Patricia was a girl in the town of Dundee, Scotland. Her parents gave her the responsibility of taking her baby twin brothers for a walk in their pram.

Crossing a busy street, she looked the wrong way, and a tramcar slammed into the children, killing them both.

Her parents blamed her for the accident, and eventually the stress over what happened resulted in her being put in a mental institution.

In this life, Patricia has always felt responsible for everyone, and when her son was diagnosed with cancer at the age of 24, she thought it had somehow been her fault. "I felt responsible—like I hadn't been careful enough," she said.

When I asked her later how knowing about this lifetime had affected her, she said, "I was immediately touched by how deeply and emotionally it resonated with me. I was able to understand the inordinate and unexplained sense of responsibility I've always felt, not only for my two sons, but for classmates or friends of my sons, too.

"Since that reading," she said, "I find that I'm able to look at my responsibilities in a much more reasonable manner. Although I continue to be very cautious with anyone in my care, I have more of an attitude that I am doing the very best that I can. I'm not so quick to immediately blame myself if anything goes wrong.

"Writing about my past life helped me to understand that the adults in that life were terribly unsupportive of me. Some people in this lifetime have also tried to put me in an undeserved defensive position.

"Now I realize I deserve compassion and understanding, and I will no longer step forward to be their 'whipping boy'. I'm also working on accepting reassurances that I'm not to blame for things that are not my fault."

ANGER = RAGE = DEATH

Certain people can be easily controlled by the threat of anger from a partner, a parent, or a boss. My client Nikki was definitely one of those. The source was a past life in Holland in which she'd died violently, hacked to death by angry soldiers.

Now, when she's around someone who might lose control of their emotions, her soul makes the following calculation: Anger = rage = death. Until we were able to empower her by dealing with the underlying past-life issue, she constantly walked on eggshells, trying to keep her volatile husband from so much as raising his voice.

Many of my clients have found the motivation to write the book they were always meant to write after speaking with my spirit guides and me. When I spoke to Kelsey, the first thing I saw in her life plan was writing. "Have you thought about writing a book," I asked.

"I've been told by all sorts of people how I should write a book," she said. "I know the story I want to share can help people, but I don't feel safe putting a book out there."

I uncovered the cause of her reluctance: a past-life fear of Self-Expression that stemmed from events in a convent on the island of Sardinia. During her time as a young novice, an older nun singled her out for attention.

The girl was sexually abused regularly for years. She blamed herself for what happened and lived in dread of God's judgment. When her parents visited her, she told them everything was fine. She went to her grave still terrified that someone would discover her shameful secret.

Kelsey's past-life fear of Self-Expression lay behind her reluctance to put her thoughts out into the world. And it manifested in another way, too. Since she was a child, doctors had never been able to explain the constant lump she'd always felt in her throat.

Immediately after our session, Kelsey sat down to journal about her past life. Suddenly, she felt a sharp pain in her throat, followed by a pop, and the lump in her throat completely disappeared. "It was incredible," she told me later. "It's totally gone."

The good news is that Kelsey is now writing and, according to my spirit guides, it's making her heart sing. "I'm working on a trilogy," she told me. "What's so incredible is that now I can share ideas with other people without crying!"

It's relatively easy to predict someone's traits, beliefs, and behavior from what happened in their past. And conversely, you can tell what happened in the past by knowing someone's traits, beliefs, and behavior in the present.

If you have an aversion to tight clothing, then it's a sign of having been restrained in a past life. I've worked with several clients who have marks on their arms where centuries ago there were iron shackles.

And if, like me, you dislike camping (my idea of roughing it is not finding a mint on my pillow when I get back to my hotel room), then you've likely been a prisoner of war or spent time in a concentration camp.

I also have an aversion to the cold. If you have constantly cold hands or feet, or dread being outside with insufficient clothing, then your soul has death from hypothermia somewhere in its past.

ABILITIES FROM THE PAST

Past-life abilities often manifest in predictable ways in the present. In the middle of a session, my client, Valerie, asked me out of the blue, "Can you tell my husband's passion in this life?"

I said, "Well, let's examine his past lives. He was once a luthier in Córdoba, in Spain. He made guitars and performed as well. And, for what it's worth, he's definitely not a Type-A personality. He must be a musician. Does he play guitar?"

She laughed and said, "He's a guitarist and singer-songwriter. And, yes, he's definitely not Type A!"

My client Lydia was born and raised in an English-speaking family in the U.S. I told her about a past life in which she'd been a French-Canadian fur trapper who froze to death when he got lost in the snow.

I asked her if she had any resonances from that past life. The kind of thing I'd expect would be extreme discomfort in the cold or a problem with cold extremities—her hands or her feet.

What she told me was quite extraordinary. One night when she was a little girl, her mother heard a strange voice coming from her daughter's bedroom. When she looked in, the room was warm, and Lydia was asleep. But she was freezing cold and her lips were blue. Not only that, but she was speaking in French.

In her sleep, Lydia had tapped into her sad and untimely death from hypothermia in the wilds of Ontario almost two hundred years ago.

Many of my clients who have experienced death in the cold have problems with their circulation or Raynaud's disease.

According to the Mayo clinic, "Doctors don't completely understand the cause of Raynaud's attacks, but blood vessels in the hands and feet appear to overreact to cold temperatures or stress." I don't imagine they've considered a past life connection.

I don't know if everyone with Raynaud's symptoms has died from hypothermia in another lifetime. But everyone I've come across who has frozen to death has cold extremities.

When I told my client Cara that she'd died from hypothermia in a run-down Moscow apartment in 1970, she said, "I can't wait for hot flashes."

MY NOT PARTICULARLY TRUE CREATION STORY

I always used to run cold, the result of death in sub-zero temperatures over two hundred years ago. So, when my children were little, I invented a story about my birth to amuse them.

"Tell us again about when you were born," they'd say.

For the umpteenth time, I'd solemnly tell them how I came into this world.

"I was born fully clothed," I'd begin.

"And tell us the bit about the 'umbiblical' cord!"

"The midwife had to unbutton my little coat and lift up my sweater so she could cut it," I'd say.

Your soul has two major blind spots. Firstly, as I mentioned earlier, it perceives all your many lives and deaths as being part of one long life. To Cara's soul, the life in Moscow was as real as this one. Her soul's discomfort with the cold had strongly influenced her decision to relocate to Florida from the midwest. It related freezing temperatures to death, and wanted to prevent her untimely demise from interrupting yet another life plan.

Secondly, your soul can't separate mind, body, and spirit, which is why an ailment like depression can cause physical illness, or why treating your body to a bubble bath and some Belgian chocolates (and I speak with a certain level of experience here) can be so emotionally and spiritually relaxing.

Though your soul can't separate one incarnation from another, the effects of past-life trauma tend to dissipate over the centuries. Most lives I explore are from the last three hundred years. But, when your soul encounters a trigger, the alarm bells start ringing, even if the original event was 1,000 years ago.

―――――

MINOR TRIGGERS, MAJOR REACTIONS

As you've seen, it doesn't take much to trigger a past-life fear. My client Donny broke up with his girlfriend after she spent a few hours in a bar with an old boyfriend. She wasn't having an affair, or even thinking about it, but his past-life fears of Betrayal and Rejection were triggered by his soul's memory of having been abandoned by his mother in 17th Century Portugal. Fortunately for both of them, the past-life exploration we did healed him in time to repair the damage and reunite with his soulmate.

―――――

PAST-LIFE HEALING IN A NUTSHELL

A major reason that past-life exploration works is that your soul can relax as soon as you remind it that whatever awful thing it fears is from another life, and no longer relevant.

It's as if your soul says, "That was a past life? Oh, right then, I'll stop worrying about it." No drama, just an awareness that history is not going to repeat itself.

Put simply, the process of healing works like this:

- Your soul encounters a reminder of past-life trauma.
- Unable to separate the past life from this life, it over-reacts to the perceived threat.
- Through past life exploration, you remind your soul that the threat is not real.
- Your soul puts the memories of events from the past back where they belong: in the past.
- You discover that problems you thought stemmed from this life actually go much further back.

Past-life fears fall into ten categories. Most people are affected by several at any one time, and their intensity can wax and wane depending on circumstances. Until a fear is healed, it will cause an imbalance, very often as a result of the soul "over-correcting" in this lifetime.

Use the following list to identify your fears by their typical cause and effect.

- **The Fear of Loss** is the result of losing loved ones, your home, or your money in a past life. It creates uncertainty about the future.
- **The Fear of Betrayal** is caused by infidelity, injustice, or disloyalty in a past life. It causes mistrust of certain people.

- **The Fear of Intimacy** is related to emotional suffering in a past life. It causes a reluctance to open your heart.
- **The Fear of Rejection** is the result of abandonment in a past life. It can show up as a tendency to isolate or a feeling you don't belong.
- **The Fear of Self-Expression** is caused by persecution for your beliefs in a past life. It creates challenges in speaking your truth.
- **The Fear of Authority** stems from being abused by authority in a past life. It will cause you to identify with the underdog.
- **The Fear of Inferiority** is the result of being treated with disdain in a past life. It will show up as low self-esteem.
- **The Fear of Powerlessness** is caused by being enslaved or imprisoned in a past life. It manifests as a strong resistance to being told what to do.
- **The Fear of Failure** is related to a disappointing or incomplete past life. It creates a lack of belief in your potential for success.
- **The Fear of Death** is the result of having caused your death, or that of others, in a past life. It shows up as a heightened responsibility for others.

Though nothing gets to the root cause of a past-life fear like regression or working with someone like me, you can start the healing process on your own. Let's say your low self-esteem suggests a past-life fear of Inferiority.

You can use this knowledge to begin exploring the cause (having been treated with disdain in a past life) by sitting quietly and simply asking your spirit guides to show you what happened.

You may start to get images, emotions, words, or a sense of what led to your problem with low self-esteem.

EXERCISE: IDENTIFY YOUR FEAR

- Find a quiet space where you won't be interrupted for five or ten minutes.
- Bring in your spirit guides and ask for protection: "I call upon my spirit guides, acting in my highest interest, to protect me at all times as I explore a significant past life. I ask you to show me the cause of my present-life problem [name it], and help me heal from its effects."
- After five or ten minutes, write any thoughts, messages, or words that come to you.

As you've seen, once you uncover the original cause of a fear or block, the present-life symptoms begin to heal, dissipate, and often disappear completely. But simply recognizing the fact that a fear without an obvious cause or one that is disproportionately extreme is from another lifetime can be enough to start the healing process—even if you don't know specifically what happened in that past life.

You'll have noticed that many of the fears and blocks related to past-life trauma show up in the body. In the next chapter, I'd like to show you how ghost memories can haunt your physical-self long after the original trauma occurred. Healing is often just a matter of bringing those memories to your consciousness.

6

ACHILLES BODY PARTS

PHYSICAL MEMORIES OF PAST LIVES

*A*n Achilles body part is an area of weakness or a place in your body where you hold physical memories of past-life trauma. I began using this term after noticing how injuries or sickness from a prior incarnation will show up in this life as a susceptibility to certain ailments or an unexplained pain in the corresponding limb or organ.

Very often an Achilles body part will fail to respond to conventional treatment or it may defy explanation. Several of my clients have told me about having exploratory surgery in an attempt to find the cause of unexplained abdominal pains. In each case, doctors were unable to discover anything because the cause was spiritual rather than physical.

I told a client once how she'd been a young man in Yugoslavia during World War II who was captured and eventually shot in both legs.

I asked her, "Do you have any unexplained pain in your legs?"

She was emphatic. "No," she said, "Nothing."

I was a little taken aback. My spirit guides were telling me specifically to ask about her legs. I didn't want to pester her, but I knew there had to be something.

"What about your ankles or your knees…"

"Oh," she said, "My knees are shot to pieces. I haven't been able to run since I was twenty."

(And, yes, she really did say, "shot to pieces.")

As with any fear from an earlier incarnation, the key to healing Achilles body parts is to remind your soul that "that was then and this is now." Often it involves little more than finding the past-life source of the ailment so that your soul can let go of the resonances it stores in your body.

TELL HIM HE SAVED MY LIFE

When Jackie called me for her third session, I heard her husband's booming voice in the background saying, "Tell him he saved my life!"

Jim was a recently retired Leader soul type that I had spoken with a few months earlier. I'd told him then that I saw a weakness from a past life in his heart chakra, and I was concerned that it was causing a physical problem.

After he replied, "My heart's in great shape," I decided not to press the point.

Fortunately, what I said inspired him to see his doctor, because it turned out there was a heart issue, and it was a miracle he was still alive. He was immediately scheduled for surgery, and had not one or two bypasses, but seven.

Before I continue, I want to be completely transparent. I've had, as you'll discover, some amazing results through the work I do. (Check out my book, *The Transformation*, or my blog site for lots of incredible examples). But I'm not a physician, and I don't make any claims to be one. I simply find out where spiritual blocks lie and by doing so, it seems to effect healing—oftentimes, dramatic healing.

And though one person may explore a past life with me and find an ailment cured by the following morning, some respond much more slowly and occasionally not at all.

I always say there are no guarantees. All we're doing is simply reminding the soul to let the ghost memories leave the body. And though healing can occur in the moment—with no apparent contribution from my client—I've found that results can be achieved by a willingness to process through writing and following other easy exercises suggested by the spirit guides.

Usually when an Achilles body part comes up in a session it's not because my client has already told me about a particular ailment or pain. Typically, I'll uncover a trauma while exploring a past life, and then ask if there's an issue in that particular area. It's my favorite part of the job.

You might be familiar with past-life regression, where someone relaxes you so you can go back to an earlier incarnation. I'll do that in a group setting, but not in a one-on-one session. In that situation, it's faster and more effective for me to simply tell a client what happened, and then explore it with them. I'm far too impatient to spend hours sitting there as someone goes, "Uh…I think I'm a girl…uh, no wait…" I'm already in the zone, and with my spirit guides' input, can uncover a past life in detail within just a few minutes.

URINATION

During a session, I told Alexandra how, as a child in France over a hundred years ago, she underwent a humiliating experience at the opera. Her mother, who was using the opportunity to hobnob with the rich and famous, refused to listen to her child's requests to use the restroom.

In the middle of the performance, the poor child was unable to hold it in any longer and urinated on the velvet opera seat. When they got home, her mother flew into a rage and beat her severely.

From that moment on, the little girl became a chronic bed-wetter. She would lie on newspapers at night and try as often as possible to sleep on the balcony outside, where losing control of her bladder didn't matter as much.

I had a very obvious question for Alexandra. "Have you ever had a problem urinating?"

"I didn't grow up with the issue as a child," she said. "The first time I came across it was when I was in college and on a 12-hour trip back to the U.S. after a Christmas holiday abroad. I needed to urinate, so I went to the bathroom while the flight was in midair and found myself unable to.

"After trying for some time, I felt self-conscious about the amount of time I'd spent in the bathroom, so I went back to my seat. I tried again later, but with no success.

"The plane then landed, and I knew that the long leg (nine hours) of the trip was still ahead. After going to the bathroom for a third time and trying with no luck again, I told the steward that I had a kidney infection and was in pain.

"I said I urgently needed to see the medical team at the airport. I was absolutely desperate. The medics whisked me off to the airport, where they hooked me up to a catheter and drained my bladder while the plane waited for me. I was mortified.

"For the next two decades, traveling, which I did several times a year, and having to use any public bathroom, such as in a restaurant, office, or someone's home, was incredibly stressful for me. I would literally dehydrate myself if I knew I was leaving the house. Road trips and flights, regardless of the length, were a nightmare.

"What's more, I then became unable to empty my bladder in one visit after that incident. The specialist told me my urethral muscle was too tight and put me on Flomax (men's prostate medication). It barely helped.

"He even stretched my urethra (which is as painful as it sounds) to improve the symptoms. It made only a slight difference."

When I next spoke to Alexandra, several years had elapsed. I asked her how things had been since we first worked together.

"To be honest," she said, "I was fascinated by what we discussed, but I never really expected it to change anything. Then one day several weeks later, I noticed that the problem had gone. Suddenly I was 95-percent better, and it's stayed that way."

"Are you able to do things now that you couldn't do before?" I asked.

"Most definitely," she said. "For example, on Wednesday I sat on a plane for a nonstop 14-hour flight and not once did this urination trauma even cross my mind. On the contrary, I now focus on hydration. I drank four medium-sized bottles of water, three cups of tea, and a coffee! What once traumatized me so much no longer even occurs to me. Thank you and the spirit guides so much."

I've pointed out many times to people like Alexandra that no one involved in a situation like this—in her case the captain and crew, the emergency medical team, or the mean-spirited passengers who blamed her for delaying the flight—would ever have thought to themselves, "Poor woman. It must be a past-life thing."

Past-life trauma like this shows up all the time in doctor's offices and hospitals. One of my clients had been shot in the leg and bled to death in Poland during WWII. Since bleeding out is the number-one cause of constipation in future lives, I asked her if that had been a problem for her. She said, "Always. My father even had to take me to the emergency room when I was a child."

CONSTIPATION: A PAST-LIFE PROBLEM

If you suffer from constipation (especially if it gets worse when you travel) and there's no obvious physiological reason for it, you might want to investigate a previous incarnation.

The original cause is loss of control in an earlier lifetime. It's most often bleeding out on a battlefield, but it can be such things as dementia, paralysis, or being bedridden.

Constipation is the result of your soul's need to clamp down on the system. And the reason it often gets worse when you travel is that your soul over-reacts when it feels outside of its comfort zone.

Some of my most appreciative clients are ones who no longer have to struggle with this uncomfortable problem.

―――――

I told a client, "You were shot in the back in your last life. Do you have a birthmark there?" (Birthmarks are often exit or entrance wounds from spears, arrows, bullets, or shrapnel.)

She said, "I do. And when I was three, I cried so much about the pain in my back, they had to take me for hospital tests―oh, and I was born with a hole in my lung!"

One of my clients bled to death in New Orleans after a knife fight almost a century ago. And when she made her one and only visit to the city in this life, simply being there triggered a huge reaction. "I hemorrhaged," she said. "It had never happened before, and it has never happened again."

When I uncover a physical injury in a past life, and I ask someone if they have a problem with unexplained abdominal pains, headaches, choking, or constipation, their reaction is often, "Yes, but I've no idea why." To which I always reply, "Well, you do now." As I'm fond of pointing out, it's not that we don't remember our past lives. We just don't know what we're looking for.

FERTILITY ISSUES

The most successful life plan is not the one where you get the biggest house, marry the most gorgeous partner, or win the lottery. It's the one in which you fulfill all, or most, of the lessons your soul set out to learn. For many of us, having children is a more important part of our life plans than our day jobs. Yet, even if your soul planned to have children, it's still possible for fear to surface and prevent conception.

If you died in childbirth in a past life, it's very likely you'll have difficulty getting pregnant in this life. The soul exerts tremendous influence over the body and will desperately try to prevent conception from happening. Vanessa came to me after having a miscarriage and no luck getting pregnant.

I told her about a particularly traumatic past life in which she'd died after having a Caesarian section with no anesthetic. Not surprisingly, she admitted to being terrified of giving birth. She left my office and I wished her well. And then I heard nothing.

I began to think things hadn't worked out until one day, about eight months later, when I got an email saying, "Update for you: I'm pregnant! I got pregnant three weeks after I met with you last December. My fear of dying in childbirth has dissipated just as your guides said it would. It's been a great pregnancy!"

The healing began the moment we uncovered the traumatic death from a lifetime several centuries ago. That allowed her soul to release its grip on her body and put the past into the past, where it belongs.

I've helped a number of women to get pregnant over the years, though, as my assistant once said, "Ainslie, you might want to find a different way of phrasing that."

MIGRAINES AND HEADACHES

In this life, Jackie was a successful CEO, until chronic, daily migraines forced her to give up her career.

It took just a few minutes to get to the root of the problem.

In the 1920s, she'd been a chauffeur in Bulgaria. On a dark road at night, he drove his employer's car into a tree. He was thrown through the windshield and died from massive head wounds.

The migraines were stress-induced ghosts of the past. When I next heard from Jackie, she was completely migraine-free and was looking forward to resuming her career.

LOSING YOUR HEAD

If you've died from hanging in a past life, you'll avoid turtlenecks and tight jewelry. It's also very likely that you'll suffer from chronic neck pain and have throat chakra issues around speaking your truth. If, however, your death was due to beheading (which turns up alarmingly often in my work) the resonance is chronic neck and shoulder pain.

During a phone session with Nancy, I discovered she'd had a life at the time of the French Revolution. She'd been a young man, a law graduate who became a magistrate and a tax collector.

When the revolution began, he worried that his wealthy background would make him a target for the angry mobs of peasants who wanted to rid France of the aristocracy, so he disguised himself and ran away.

Unfortunately, he was exposed by his manners and accused of being an aristocrat. During his arrest and imprisonment, his hands and cheekbones were broken. Adding to his discomfort, he was held in a cellar with metal restraints around his legs, which caused painful skin irritation. On his way to the guillotine, he was led through a mob of jeering citizens before finally having his head cut off.

I asked Nancy if she'd ever had a problem with her neck and shoulders.

"I've had twenty years of chronic pain," she said. "To make matters worse, I'm a ballroom-dance teacher. I'm continually having to turn my head." I assured her that it wouldn't take too long for her soul to release the memory and for healing to begin.

Well, as we spoke, the pain lifted—literally in that moment—and it has never returned.

Throughout her life, Nancy also suffered from a host of other irrational problems stemming from that past life. Having been exposed—having her disguise seen through—she hates being in the public eye. On one occasion, she lost her normally mellow demeanor when a friend innocently posted a picture of her on Facebook.

The damage to her hands has translated to pains in her wrists and what she describes as her thumbs being "cranky." The memory of her broken cheekbone shows itself as intermittent jaw pain.

She also has skin issues on her legs where there were once iron restraints and she can't wear any metal—jewelry, or a watch—against her skin. She can't bear any weight on the back of her neck. In fact, she told me she thought she might have been in the stocks in a past life.

And after such a cruel death, she has a massive sense of fairness and justice. The ridicule she encountered on her way to the gallows has also left its mark. She'd always been afraid of crowds and the mob mentality, and she couldn't bear to be teased.

In early 2014, I taught a workshop at East West Bookstore in Seattle. I told the audience about Nancy's traumatic past life in

Revolutionary France. At the back of the room, a woman put her hand up and said, "That was me!"

I've met Nancy two more times since then, and her chronic neck and shoulder pain has never returned. All we had to do to create lasting healing was to remind her soul that the stress it was holding onto came from a lifetime hundreds of years ago.

And now Nancy is able to fully embrace her destiny as a dance teacher, without every turn of her neck sending jolts of pain through her body. Her life plan is finally in full swing.

PANIC ATTACKS

As someone who once suffered debilitating panic attacks, I have a lot of compassion for those who have to deal with such effects.

One evening, a few years ago, I was preparing for a weekend workshop at Kripalu, a large retreat center in Massachusetts. With twenty minutes to go before meeting the attendees for the first time, I was alone in the classroom. Out of the corner of my eye, I noticed a man in loose-fitting white pajamas standing in the doorway.

I gave him a smile, as he walked silently towards me. All of a sudden, he dropped to his knees and began wailing, "I am dying! You must help me, I am dying..."

I didn't know what to say. In a few minutes forty people would be turning up, expecting my full attention. I helped him to his feet assuring him (with less than total confidence) that if he simply followed the program over the next few days, he'd be as right as rain at the end of it.

"Are you in the U.S. for long?" I asked, trying to lighten things up a bit.

"No," he said, "I have come from New Delhi for the weekend. I have come for you to heal me!" He told me how he hadn't eaten for three days and that he'd had ten panic attacks during the previous night.

I was torn. I really wanted to help the poor fellow. But I also felt a responsibility to the others. And as they began trickling into the room, I urged him to take a seat and assured him everything would be just fine. He sat through the next 90 minutes in obvious discomfort, occasionally clutching his head and letting out a moan.

Once the room emptied, he resumed the kneeling position and continued begging me for help. Since the course I was teaching involved healing traumatic past lives to deal with phobias and other blocks, I just repeated what I'd already told him.

We went through a similar ritual the next morning. After more tears, and more impassioned requests for me to "bless" him, I was starting to worry that he'd become a major disruption to the class.

Kumar sat right at the front, just feet from me. His face, and the occasional groan, revealed the anguish he was still going through. Every so often, he'd begin hyperventilating.

After he had another major panic attack, I accepted that his needs were a priority. When the class ended, I set about uncovering the cause of his misery.

According to my spirit guides it was all very simple. In a past life in 1930's New York, he was a boy whose father took him to a picket line. When mounted police attacked the striking workers, he was crushed under the weight of the crowd.

I sat Kumar down and told him what had happened to him. He stared into the distance as I reminded his soul of the events from long ago. Then he looked me in the eye and said, "I need to eat." And off he went.

I saw Kumar again an hour later. He was smiling and full of energy. He told me couldn't believe the change he felt inside. Once again, he fell to the floor in front of me, but this time he was simply overwhelmed with gratitude.

To ensure I'd have the opportunity to monitor his progress, I offered the class a prize—a session with me—for the person who had traveled furthest to be there. No one, of course, could beat New Delhi.

When I spoke to Kumar a month or two later, he described how the panic attacks cleared up the moment I told him about the past life. In fact, he'd felt so much better that he'd decided to visit a relative in Manhattan before returning to India.

He had a minor panic attack on arriving in the city, but it quickly subsided. Given that New York was the scene of the original trauma, it wasn't surprising that his soul would feel some trepidation.

Panic attacks are a past-life fear of Loss of Control, the result of events in your soul's past in which you lost control of your body. In Kumar's case, it was what happened when he was being crushed to death in a state of extreme fear.

PHYSICIAN, HEAL THYSELF

Unexplained pains and mysterious aches are often physical resonances from past-life trauma. And sometimes, they'll show up unexpectedly when I'm working with someone.

During a session, I told a client that she'd had her right eye gouged out in a past life. She let out a yelp, not because it was such a shocking thing to hear, but because ten seconds earlier she'd experienced a stabbing pain behind her right eye.

In another session, my client—a woman in this life—had been a young man in Hollywood during the silent movie era. Down on his luck, he had stolen a wallet from a wealthy businessman who shot him in the hip as he tried to run away. A second before I told her the location of the bullet wound, she grabbed her hip and let out a very loud "Ow!"

Why did those two clients suddenly have stabbing pains during their sessions? It's because time is fluid on the other side, and that means your soul often experiences events before they happen. (That's why you sometimes know who's on the line before you answer the phone, or why you might feel anxiety hours before receiving bad news.)

Before I told my clients what happened, their souls were already recalling the trauma.

IN A ROOM OF A HUNDRED PEOPLE...

I have several clients who hide knives. Nicole was stabbed in a past life, and told me how if anyone in her family wants a knife or a razor blade, they have to come to her for one.

Gerry's past life involved the murder of her parents. During the Franco-Prussian War of 1870, they refused to hand over food to soldiers and were cut down with swords. Now Gerry hides sharp knives.

Monica doesn't hide them, but she described how she can't walk by a sharp knife. In an earlier incarnation, she'd been slashed by a jealous lover when she resisted his advances. It explained why, when she was younger and a boyfriend threatened to cut his wrists with a razorblade, she collapsed on the floor in a state of complete hysterics.

In a room of a hundred people, I doubt anyone would have the extreme reactions to sharp blades seen in these three.

In my line of work, I'm used to weird things happening. But one of the oddest occurred when I was exploring a routine past life (if routine is a word you can apply to such things) with Elizabeth.

"You joined the British Army and were posted to India," I told her. "Not long after arriving there, you died from tetanus—lockjaw...Ow!"

The moment I said the word "tetanus," I experienced an excruciating pain in my jaw. It ran from my temples down both sides of my face to my chin and spread down to the top of my chest.

Initially, I thought that my spirit guides were giving me some kind of empathic experience. My client recalls me exclaiming, "I get it!" and "That's enough!" She thought my guides and I were arguing. Meanwhile, my heart was pounding as I struggled to suppress a feeling of intense panic.

The worst of the pain subsided after a minute or so. I was left with a dull ache and a slight constriction in my throat. At the end of the session, I apologized to my client for all the drama and moved on to my next appointment, without having the opportunity to discuss what happened with my guides.

I shared with my next client what had just happened. But when I uttered the word "tetanus," the pain came back almost instantly. It wasn't quite as intense as before, but enough to cause my heart to race and the muscles in my jaw to clench.

My next call that day was with a doctor client. Again, I shared what had happened. The moment I said the "T" word, the pain enveloped my jaw once more. "It sounds like a past-life issue to me," he said.

And, sure enough, it was. When I finally had a few minutes to check in, I asked my spirit guides what was going on. It was far from some overblown empathic reaction. I had stumbled upon a past-life issue of my own. Elizabeth's past-life death in India mirrored my own death in America during the same period.

I had my guides take me back into a life in the Carolinas, where I'd been a barefoot boy living on a farm. I jumped down from a hayloft, cutting my toe on some rusty farm implements. I contracted tetanus and died in extreme pain not long after.

The session with Elizabeth had triggered a deep memory within my soul. Once I'd explored that particular life and death, however, the ache in my jaw dissipated and has never returned, no matter how often I use the words "tetanus" or "lockjaw."

After we uncovered her prior incarnation in India, I asked if she had issues with her jaw. It was not surprising to hear that she did. Her jaw would lock in the dentist's chair, causing her extreme distress.

Since we explored that past life together, however, she's had no problems with her jaw. And neither have I. (In the past, I'd cracked two molars from clenching my jaw, prompting my dentist to ask me, "What's the matter? Don't you like your teeth?")

DYING BY THE SWORD

I've often been asked questions like, "Can you tell me why my left shoulder hurts?" I've come across a number of people in my work who have unexplained pain in the left side of their body.

In a world in which most people are right-handed, the past-life source of these Achilles body parts turns out to be injuries inflicted by right-handed punches or right-handed swordsmen in battle.

INFLEXIBILITY

Working with 26-year old Michelle, I uncovered a particularly traumatic past life death. She'd been a Chinese male who was captured by Japanese soldiers, forced into a tiny wicker basket, and left to die in the sun.

I expected she'd have some significant stiffness in her body after dying in such a cramped position. What she told me was astonishing.

She's suffered from chronic neck and back pain all her life. She's never had any flexibility. As a figure skater, it impacted her ability to do certain moves and spins. She never saw a doctor, because she chalked it up to genetics.

I told her she'd probably get almost instant relief from the pain in her neck and back. And, sure enough, healing began within 24 hours.

The pain had begun to lift by the next day, so she bent over to touch her toes. She'd never in her life made it beyond her knees, but this time she was able to reach her ankles.

Michelle wrote to me saying, "It's amazing! To most people it wouldn't seem like a big difference, but I'm amazed by the change. I do it a few times a day now, just to see if it's real!" (Fortunately, such healing always seems to be permanent.)

Two days after I worked with Michelle, I had a session with her mother, Ruth. She told me that Michelle had been sending her pictures of herself showing off her newfound flexibility.

Like most people seeking to understand the cause of an aliment, Ruth never thought of it being a past-life issue, and had always put her daughter's neck and back pain down to years of carrying heavy textbooks at school.

She said, "When Michelle sent the photo of her almost touching her toes, I couldn't believe it! This was a very dramatic change—and only one day after her session with you."

And just so she wouldn't feel left out, I found a past life in which Ruth had been beheaded. Not surprisingly, she's carried a lot of neck and shoulder pain with her in this life.

I checked in with her at the end of the session and asked her how the pain was. She said, "Wow, I can't feel anything!" A few days later she emailed to say that she, too, had experienced tremendous relief from her pain.

EXERCISE: IDENTIFY YOUR ACHILLES BODY PARTS

Achilles body parts include headaches, digestive problems, chronic pain, and pretty much anything that doesn't have an obvious cause. Do you have a particular area of your body that always seems to be a problem? Do colds start or settle in a particular place, like your throat or lungs? Do you have a pain or recurring problem that doctors can't explain?

- List three areas of weakness or chronic pain in your body.
- Using your intuition, list three possible past-life causes for your Achilles body parts.
- Spend some time writing about these past lives. Don't try to edit, just write. The more time you spend simply allowing the words to flow, the easier it will be to get out of your conscious mind and tap into your soul's past so you can experience a release of the painful past-life resonance.

An Achilles body part, as you've seen, is a ghost of the past. It can prevent you from living up to your potential. Like the crate in which Michelle was held captive back in her life in China, you can be trapped by an Achilles effect until your soul recognizes it as something from another incarnation.

But you may well find yourself inside another box. It's one created and imposed on you by others, and it can cause you to go through this life carrying limiting beliefs that quite simply don't belong to you.

7

LIVING YOUR OWN LIFE

ESCAPING THE EXPECTATIONS OF OTHERS

From the moment you come into this life, people will want to change you. And that's what, more than almost anything else, will take you off your life plan. Some do it willfully to control you. Others are simply unaware that by imposing their expectations on you, they risk derailing your life plan.

When you were a baby, you would have manifested your soul type and influences quite strongly. For example, if you happened to be a Hunter type with a Performer influence, you might have given that away by your robust rambunctiousness and the way you couldn't listen to music without swinging your hips.

On the deepest level, no one knows you better than you know yourself. Your life plan is carried by your soul into this life. The problem, of course, is being able to access, or remember, your life plan once your soul takes human form again.

Actually, the even bigger problem is that very few of us had parents who recognized that we were something more than a chip off the old block. For example, when you were little, did someone ever ask you why you couldn't be more like your grandfather, your brother or sister, a deceased relative, or the kid next-door?

It's a fact of life, that from the moment you take your first breath, other people impose their expectations upon you. Not surprisingly, mom and dad are the worst culprits. But, as you grow up, the expectations that your parents have for you get added to by those of teachers, your peers, society, and just about anyone you can think of.

Those expectations may be positive, like assuming you'll go to college after high school. But they can also reflect another person's fears or limiting beliefs.

Sonia told me how her father raised her to believe that she was incapable of doing anything for herself. Knowing that about her, would you expect her to have simply ignored his discouragement and been able to stick to her life plan, or do you think she might have had some challenges in that area?

I think you know the answer. The influence of parents can be enormous. And their expectations can stick with us throughout our lives, even if we're not consciously aware of them.

Another client, Thomas, grew up being discouraged from expressing his emotions. His father was a military officer, and his mom grew up in a family where emotions were suppressed. His parents' unconscious expectation was that their child would be like them.

But he wasn't. Thomas is a more gentle, sensitive soul—a Creator type. As a child, he was criticized harshly for crying or complaining. He learned to bottle up his feelings and to never reveal how he truly felt about anything. When I first worked with him, his blocked emotions were playing havoc with his relationship. And, because the true Thomas was a touchy-feely kind of guy, his stoic behavior caused him to come across as inauthentic. As he put it, "I don't really know who I am."

WHEN THE TRUE YOU IS NOT ACCEPTABLE

Your soul type is your essence, the very heart of who you are. And when your family of origin demands you be something else, it's an attack on your soul.

Each soul type can be described in pejorative terms. These are some typical examples of the messages each soul type will hear at some point in their lives:

- **The Helper Type**: You're not ambitious enough
- **The Caregiver Type**: You're too giving
- **The Educator Type**: You're such a know-it-all
- **The Thinker Type**: You're too cerebral
- **The Creator Type**: You're too sensitive
- **The Performer Type**: You're too attention-seeking
- **The Hunter Type**: You're too aggressive
- **The Leader Type**: You're too bossy
- **The Spiritualist Type**: You're too idealistic
- **The Transformer Type**: You're always causing trouble

Many parents expect their children to behave in a way that's contrary to their true personality. The world is full of Creators who grew up hearing they needed to toughen up, Caregivers who were mocked for always feeling other people's pain, or crying about the mistreatment of animals, and Thinkers who were criticized for not expressing their feelings more.

Then there are Hunters who were ordered to sit down and stop jumping around, Helpers who were told they should have more drive, Educators who were accused of talking too much, and Performers who were put down for showing off.

Not to mention all the Leaders who were called bossy, Spiritualists who were mocked for their bleeding hearts, and even the occasional Transformer who was reminded, "You can't change the world."

How different might the world be if we were all appreciated for our innate qualities, instead of being made to feel there's something wrong with us? It can be immensely useful to look back on your childhood and ask yourself if any negative beliefs about who you are stand up to scrutiny.

These descriptors can also help you with identifying your Soul Types and Influences in the exercise at the end of Chapter 4.

EXPECTATIONS AND KARMA

I want to address the topic of karma because it has a very significant bearing on expectations. To put it very simply, if you have unreasonable or selfish expectations of someone, there can be a karmic consequence.

Let's say that you're the parent and you want your child to be an engineer, but the child came into this world to be a ballet dancer. Imagine the child is five years old, and says, "For my birthday next week, I'd like a ballet tutu."

If you say, "You're not getting a ballet tutu; I'm buying you an adjustable wrench," then you might well be imposing your expectations on them. Maybe you wanted to be a mechanic when you were a kid, and now you're trying to live vicariously through your own child. Or maybe you want them to grow up to be like Uncle Phil who runs an auto shop.

If your child grows up to be a ballet dancer, they might look back on their fifth birthday with a laugh, saying, "I can't believe they thought I would be an engineer!" In that case, little damage is done.

But so many children grow up to follow paths that were chosen for them, even if the encouragement from parents, teachers, or others was subtle. They end up, like many of the people who come to me for help, worn out from spending eight hours a day under fluorescent lighting, feeding the corporate monster they despise.

They know life has something more important in store for them, but they can't figure out what that is because they never had the chance to truly be themselves.

No soul wants to wind up on its deathbed regretting not having done the things it longed to. As I mentioned before, there are few things worse for old souls than to have missed out on fulfilling their life plans.

YOU'RE SMART, YOU SHOULD BE A DOCTOR

I work with a lot of physicians. Almost all of them were meant to be doctors, and are old-soul Spiritualist types seeking ways to heal others. But several of my doctor clients stand out. While they're excellent at what they do, medicine was never meant to be their career.

One became a doctor instead of a classical musician because of the influence of her father. Another because teachers thought his impressive grades meant he could become a doctor and make piles of money. Most of them agreed with me when I suggested they might transition into other work at some point.

If the expectation you impose on your child takes them radically off their life plan, your soul—recognizing that what you've done has incurred karma—will urge you to rectify the situation and start supporting their true purpose as quickly as possible. Otherwise, you may have to spend time in future incarnations making up for what you did to derail that person's life plan.

I'M NOT GOOD ENOUGH

When Valerie was a child, her dad pinched her flesh and said, "You're a little porker, aren't you?" For the next four decades she saw herself as the little porker. Her father's throwaway comment had triggered a past-life fear of Inferiority and the limiting belief, "I'm not good enough."

Like a lot of people who feel inadequate, she settled for less in her relationships, believing that she was not good enough to be worthy of one that was healthy and loving.

Valerie's father and siblings judged her by her appearance. But because she was overweight, not particularly athletic, and didn't get the dates her sisters did, she accepted the label they gave her.

Thanks to the combination of a past-life fear of Inferiority (not wanting to appear lesser) and a past-life fear of Judgment (hypersensitivity to criticism), she was an academic overachiever. However, when she graduated from college and was offered several jobs, she chose the one that was least challenging and paid the least.

Then she met the guy who became her first husband and put up with appalling behavior from him. On a soul-deep level, she didn't feel she deserved anything better because of her "fundamental flaw."

Significantly, when she tried to quit smoking, her siblings taunted her by smoking in front of her and continually offering her cigarettes. And when she dieted, they made fun of her, rather than supporting her.

They knew her a certain way. They didn't want her escaping from the confines of her limiting belief to become healthier, more confident, and happier. That's not to say that they didn't love her, but that they didn't feel comfortable when she stepped out of her self-limiting box.

The question here is: has anyone said or done something that made you feel you're not good enough? Did parents, teachers, siblings, or anyone else determine that you were inadequate in some way? And if they did, is that your belief now, or is it time to let it go?

OTHERS KNOW BEST

When parents, teachers, priests, or others in a position of authority tell you they know what's best for you, there's a problem.

Although it's important to have older and wiser individuals to look to for direction as you grow up, the danger is that you continue to believe they are the greater authority.

Like Molly, you might be 40 years old and still running every decision past mom and dad. That was fine when she was ten, but when she ditched her boyfriend because mom and dad felt he wouldn't make a good father, she allowed their beliefs to become hers (when in reality, the relationship was a soul agreement).

She wasn't seeking their approval; she genuinely saw them as having some kind of insight she lacked.

Molly's parents are not likely to stop giving their two-cents worth anytime soon. They get to feel they play an important part in her life. But when they're gone, she's going to struggle to make her own decisions.

At work, Molly's challenge is that she defers to others. Because she lacks sufficient recognition of her own abilities, she won't seek a promotion, a better job, or anything that might elevate her in the eyes of others.

At the end of our first session together, Molly asked, "When should I schedule another session with you?" I'm pleased to say she laughed when I told her, "You decide." Simply being aware that she needs to listen to her intuition and make her own decisions, she's on track to take her life in a far healthier and empowered direction.

REACHING OUT TO OTHERS

There's a big difference between asking someone for their input because you want to make sure you're all on the same page and looking for their approval to determine your next move. When you check out a decision with others, always ask yourself if you're seeking consensus or approval.

I AM UNDESERVING

Did anyone ever tell you that you were ungrateful or that you should count your blessings? That's what my wife, Christine, grew up hearing from her Depression–era father. He frequently told her, "Take what they give you and don't ask for more."

It's a statement that revealed an enormous amount about his fears, the biggest being one of Loss, which came from a past life in which he'd suffered severe deprivation. The trigger in this life was, of course, his impoverished upbringing during the Great Depression of the 1930s.

If, as a child you're always told that you're ungrateful, as an adult you may feel it's somehow wrong to seek more than you have or to attempt to better yourself in some way.

You may be someone who says, "I'm not happy with the way things are, but I should be grateful for what I have." It's one of the reasons so many people end up trapped in a miserable relationship or career. They feel they should just suck it up and not complain. If you ask, "How's work?" they answer, "Not great, but at least it's a job."

It's important to be grateful for what you have, but not if it prevents you from wanting to improve your life. I'm pleased to say that Christine recognized the limitations of this belief and has since made sure her father's fear didn't become her own.

THERE'S NOTHING I CAN DO ABOUT IT

If others teach you that you're helpless to change anything, they disempower you. The expectation imposed on you is that you should accept that life sucks and that you're powerless to do anything about it. In your family of origin, the message might've been that life is not fair, so you have no expectations you can change it. A stereotypical 1950's dad might well have expressed it as, "You can't fight City Hall."

The feeling of being helpless against external forces is the result of a past-life fear of Powerlessness being triggered. Julia grew up watching her father bully her mother. Her mom never stood up for herself and, like a lot of abused spouses, made excuses for him. Unfortunately, the message Julia got was one of disempowerment.

Julia was going through a dispute with a collection agency over debt incurred by her ex-husband. She was prepared to part with a pretty big chunk of change until we explored the reason for her passivity. We did some past-life work, too and, not long afterwards, she came to a much more reasonable financial settlement.

Do you ever feel that there's no real point in trying to change anything because it's just the way things are? Be mindful of this kind of thinking, because you don't want to fall into victim mentality. It's always worth examining whether you're really as powerless as you think.

RECOGNIZING YOUR POWER

Your soul never wants to stay in a place of victimization. It will always urge you to stand up for yourself, whether you're being pushed around by a partner, controlled by a superior at work, or at the mercy of your sweet tooth. When it comes to changing a situation that isn't serving you, the spirit guides say, "Everyone has more power than they recognize. Everyone."

OTHER PEOPLE GET ALL THE LUCK

Ron's father relocated the family from Mexico to California when the kids were young. But the job he'd been promised failed to materialize. Instead of finding another one, he left the country (and his family) and went back home. Ron's dad taught his son that success was something other people achieved, not blue-collar immigrants like them.

Ron was successful as a recording engineer until work became sporadic. Instead of redoubling his efforts to keep his career going, he took a job on a trawler in Alaska (not something that was consistent with his life plan). He bailed out and left his wife and their young daughter, just as his father had done to Ron's mother and her children thirty years earlier.

If you believe that you'll never really amount to anything, or that success is for other people, then that will become your reality. This is a manifestation of the past-life of Failure and is made worse every time something doesn't work out as planned in this lifetime.

Multiple disappointments tend to reinforce the belief that

success is for others—not you. Over time, this can even lead to the belief that you're fated or somehow doomed to never achieving your goals.

The belief that success can never be attained is one that can end up being passed down through generations. It is, however, something that can be released through past-life healing work. And even if you don't know the past-life cause, healing can begin when you recognize it for what it is: a limiting belief.

IT'S NOT SAFE TO OPEN MY HEART

Shauna's mother raised her to believe that men were useless creatures and that sex was something to be endured for procreation only. It didn't surprise me to hear her criticize her current boyfriend for having lost his mojo the night before after she told him, "Hurry up, I have an early start in the morning." And it certainly wasn't shocking to hear how her relationships with men never lasted more than a few months.

The fear of intimacy is a past-life issue and almost always suggests there's been rape or sexual abuse in the soul's recent incarnations. Shauna's mother clearly had the fear, but I couldn't uncover any obvious cause for it in her own life, past or present. (Which is unusual because, unfortunately, you rarely have to scratch too deeply to find an unhealed past life of sexual abuse.) It looked like her mother's fear had become hers.

Her mother's belief was that love is scary because it makes you vulnerable and that a relationship can never be truly satisfying. "My mother and I often say we wish we could live in a world without men," Shauna told me.

It's worth mentioning that Shauna was meant to be in an intimate relationship. Her soul craved intimacy, but the fear she'd adopted caused her to push it away. Telling her boyfriend to hurry up and get it over with was one of a hundred ways of sabotaging things so she wouldn't have to risk facing the vulnerability that comes with intimacy.

If a parent (or anyone else, for that matter) imposes their cynical beliefs about love on you, there's a coda you can use to help complete their sentences. It looks like this: When they say, as Shauna's mother did, "Men—they're all the same," or "You're better off without a relationship," you can simply add, "...in your opinion." Even silently completing their words will help remind you that their beliefs are not necessarily yours.

I'd like to report that Shauna is completely healed now, but unfortunately, I can't. Her one and only session with me ended with her defending her mother's beliefs as if they were her own. "You don't understand," she said, "You're not a woman." It's true, I'm not. However, in this case, it wasn't about gender differences, but rather an example of how hard it can be to question or release our deeply-held beliefs, even when they don't serve us.

YOU WON'T LIKE ME WHEN YOU GET TO KNOW ME

As a child, were you expected to always be nice or well behaved to the point where you had to cover up your true feelings? Did you have to be something you were not to please the grown-ups in your life? If you had to hide the real you when you were a child, the risk is that you'll continue doing it as an adult.

Souls seek to understand one another. It's why young (or even old) lovers stare into each other's eyes. Each soul is saying, "I want to see who you are, and I want you to see me."

If you've learned to be someone you're not, the message you'll give another person will be incongruous. What they see will not necessarily be consistent with what they feel. Sometimes, they might not even want to be around you.

And if that happens, you might be forgiven for thinking you just need to try harder, rather than recognizing the need to be more authentic. The programming you got as a child will then cause you to double down on your "niceness," which will only make things worse.

The belief that a more aggressive girl (like a Hunter type) should be passive and gentle, and a more sensitive boy (like a Creator type) should be more aggressive, is common in this culture. If you have a pre-existing past-life condition like a fear of Self-Expression, you might struggle all your life between the need to be yourself and the sense that being yourself is not enough.

I'D BETTER DO WHAT I'M TOLD

Some parents and teachers use coercion to create obedience. If you were the obedient child of coercive parents, the risk is that you'll continue to allow other people to coerce you. This is related to the past-life fear of Rejection, often stemming from once having been abandoned or sometimes from having died alone.

If you're coerced into doing anything, it means you're not making a choice with free will, and that can quickly lead to you being taken off your life plan. The draft, conscription into the military, is an example of coercion that often leads to death.

I've seen many a client with a degree in business—rather than something like art—because of parental pressure. One told me that her father refused to pay for college if she left the Chicago area.

On a soul level, the inability to resist being coerced stems from a need for love. And that's why a past-life of abandonment (which causes a fear of Rejection) will make you so ready to comply. The implication behind coercion is that if you don't do what you're told, you'll lose the approval—and therefore the love—of the person who is controlling you.

That's why so many of us can be controlled or coerced

through anger, rage, or violence. It causes many children to walk on eggshells trying to keep mom or dad happy.

A child who learns not to express their anger or how to say no becomes a victim for abusers of all kinds. As they grow up, their avoidance of conflict can lead them to become prey for bullies in every walk of life.

In a session, a client told me that the fear of her husband's anger made her passive in her marriage. She would conform to her partner's expectations because she felt it could be dangerous to do otherwise. I asked her, "Has he ever been physically violent towards you?" She answered, "No, but I think he could."

Coercion is a form of aggression, and aggression towards another human is contrary to every soul's desire for peace. A person who uses aggression to control another human being creates a karmic debt that must be resolved in future lifetimes.

LIFE IS TOO SHORT

Barb is a Level 10 soul and in her early seventies. Since this is most likely her last life on earth, her soul doesn't want to waste any time.

During a session, Barb complained that someone she hadn't seen for years had invited her to stay with her. The trip involved a long air flight followed by an equally long drive, and this person had treated her badly in the past.

She didn't want to go and had a lot of other things she'd rather do. But her friend is easily hurt and she didn't want to upset her.

With gentle humor, the spirit guides told her, "Your soul would rather go to Disneyland. And that's its idea of hell!"

To help empower Barb, the spirit guides gave her a mantra

they promised would create a positive shift: "I will no longer hurt myself to please someone else."

I encourage you to use this phrase if you find yourself unable to say no to people for fear of hurting their feelings.

WHAT IF I MAKE THE WRONG DECISION?

Jeff had a past life in which he caused his own death by crashing a plane during training in England during World War II. It was entirely his fault. That fact alone would have made him predisposed to second-guessing every decision in this life under the best of circumstances.

But in his current life, Jeff's family undermined him even further by continually pointing out his mistakes and criticizing his decisions. By the time he came to me, he'd suffered 35 years of parental disapproval.

When he was five years old, he lost his beloved teddy bear in the park. His father said, "You always do that," a statement that has puzzled Jeff ever since, given that he'd never knowingly lost a teddy bear (or anything else) before then.

He remembered, too, how his mother would always have him change his clothes before going out. If he wore the blue sweater, she'd have him change into the green one.

As an adult, Jeff was hesitant to make any decision, small or large. When I first spoke to him, he'd just separated from his wife, but was keeping the news from his parents for fear he'd be reminded that he always messed things up.

Things improved rapidly after our session because, as Jeff put it, "Your spirit guides helped me to realize I hadn't screwed up, but that it's the nature of life that things don't always work out as you expected. It was something I really needed to hear."

MY NEEDS ARE NOT IMPORTANT

My spirit guides once asked me, "Why do humans say, 'I have no expectations?'" I hazarded a guess or two, but they continued, "Because souls have expectations."

From the moment your soul arrives in a new body, it has strong expectations. The soul of the parent or parents will have made an agreement with the soul of the baby to nurture and protect it. And that's the expectation.

Whether there are two parents or only one, or if there are two moms or two dads, or if the baby is adopted, the expectation is still the same.

If your mother didn't love you, failed to nurture you, or left you to your own devices, it would be considered a betrayal of expectations and that would have triggered a past-life fear of Betrayal.

And if that meant you had to be significantly self-reliant, the message your soul would have received was that its needs were not important.

You'll see this in latchkey kids. And it's often strong in someone who as a child was expected to take care of their younger siblings or had to pretty much raise themselves. Their soul learned that when it comes down to it, "There's only one person I can count on and that's me."

Many souls, anticipating the need to be highly independent, will choose a mission of Reliance as part of their life plan. (This is actually the same mission a soul might select if their life is one in which they'll always have to rely on others. Reliance and self-reliance are two sides of the same coin.)

In doing so, they deliberately tap into a prior incarnation called an "orphan life." This is one in which the soul was forced, often through abandonment, to go it alone. The energy of self-reliance can then be harnessed in this life.

I CAN ONLY RELY ON MYSELF

A mission of Reliance in a person's life plan is a two-way street. It can be used when life circumstances make it necessary to either rely heavily on others or on yourself.

When I spotted extreme self-reliance in one client, I asked her, "Were you a particularly independent little girl?"

She said, "I tried to change my own diaper. How's that?"

It seems ironic that when you're raised by a disinterested, unloving, unavailable, or detached parent, they may have very strong expectations that you'll be the one to look after them when they get old. It puts the child in a tricky position. On one hand, they carry deep mistrust, but on the other, a deep sense of loyalty.

If it's your belief that "my needs are not important," it's vital to make sure you nurture yourself and question your obligations to others. You must make sure you don't put others' needs ahead of your own, especially if it's to your detriment.

ESCAPING THE BOX

The influence of your family of origin can put you in a box of their making. But once you can separate their beliefs from yours, you'll recognize that the only person keeping you in the box is you.

When clients tell me that their family disapproves of how they quit a safe career to follow their true calling, or how their spouses disparage their spiritual interests, I often tell them the following story.

Many years ago, I was on a visit to my family in Scotland,

when I came out of the closet about my chosen path as a psychic. My brother is someone with whom I'm very close, but spirituality is a topic on which we differ. I waited until we were alone in a pub to tell him.

"I've decided to give up illustration to be a full-time psychic," I said.

He peered over a pint of lager, looked me straight in the eye, and asked, with mock sincerity, "So what's your website then, barkingfuckingmad.com?"

And that was about as far as we got that night. We see the world differently and that's just fine. To expect him to share my perspective was simply unrealistic.

I did however take something positive from our exchange, which is why barkingfuckingmad.com links to my main website.

If you live your life according to the worldview of others instead of your own, you're not going to look back from your deathbed pleased that you did so.

It's worth pointing out that it can be comforting to have the approval of those you love, but it should never be something that stops you from living your own authentic life.

When limiting beliefs are imposed on you, your past-life fears are easily triggered. For example, being told you're not good enough can trigger your past-life fear of Inferiority (from lives where you were treated as lesser).

When certain past-life fears are triggered, you risk becoming disempowered. A fear of Inferiority can easily do this by reinforcing your soul's pre-existing belief that you're not worthy.

Healing a fear like this is enhanced through past-life exploration. That way, you get to the core of the problem. You can also make huge shifts in your life by simply noticing the limiting beliefs when they surface and replacing them with a positive message. Combining the two approaches will help even more.

EXERCISE: EMPOWERING BELIEFS

Take a look at the following ten self-limiting beliefs. Find the ones that resonate with you. Then replace them with positive empowering beliefs that you can use as affirmations or mantras. Choose ones from the list below or create your own. You might, for example, replace the limiting belief "I'm not good enough" with "I'm just as good as everybody else."

- **Limiting Belief:** I'm not good enough
- **Empowering Statement:** I'm perfect just the way I am

- **Limiting Belief:** Others know best
- **Empowering Statement**: I'm capable of making my own choices

- **Limiting Belief:** I am undeserving
- **Empowering Statement:** I'm worthy of abundance in my life

- **Limiting Belief:** There's nothing I can do about it
- **Empowering Statement:** I refuse to be victimized by anyone or anything

- **Limiting Belief:** Other people get all the luck
- **Empowering Statement:** I have as much right to success as anyone else

- **Limiting Belief:** It's not safe to open my heart
- **Empowering Statement:** I deserve to love and be loved

- **Limiting Belief:** You won't like me once you get to know me
- **Empowering Statement:** I'm proud to be myself

- **Limiting Belief:** I'd better do what I'm told
- **Empowering Statement:** I will not hurt myself to please others

- **Limiting Belief:** What if I make the wrong decision?
- **Empowering Statement:** I trust my ability to make wise choices

- **Limiting Belief:** My needs are not important
- **Empowering Statement:** I deserve to have my needs met

Incorporate the empowering statements into your daily meditations, or simply repeat them a few times when you recognize you're slipping into old patterns of belief. And if you're not sure which empowering statement is most appropriate, simply repeat the following phrase three times: "I refuse to allow other people's limiting beliefs to become my own."

This is your life and it should be lived on your terms. If someone interferes with your life plan, then say or do something to set a boundary for yourself. Follow your intuition. Do what feels right for you. Anything else risks incurring karma, and that's something, as you'll see, you want to avoid.

8

KILL AND BE KILLED

KARMIC CONSEQUENCES

*O*f all the concepts that come up in my work, I believe that karma is the most misunderstood, especially since every one of us is significantly affected by it. So what is karma and how does it really work?

For some, karma implies "an eye for an eye" or some kind of divine retribution (you squished a cockroach and now you're doomed to return as a bug). Many believe that karma is punishment (when bad things happen, you're being punished for wrongdoings committed in a previous incarnation).

Well, let's be clear. According to my spirit guides, there is no such thing as divine punishment. There is no vengeful supreme being planning to banish you to purgatory because you prayed to the wrong god, cheated, lied, stole, abused, played the bagpipes, or committed any other indiscretion. There is, quite simply, no punishment.

There's no divine punishment for killing either. It doesn't matter whether you were Adolf Hitler or some downtrodden foot soldier who had to shoot the other guy to save his own life. No matter what the circumstance, there is no punishment. (I know it seems shocking but read on and I'll explain.)

Does this mean you can slaughter as many as you like and get away with it? Definitely not. There may be no spiritual punishment, but there is karma. And when it comes to karma, you can run, but you most certainly can't hide.

So, if karma is not punishment, what is it? Think of karma as the universe's way of balancing the experience of one event with that of another.

If you killed people in a past life, do you let them kill you sometime in the future? The answer is no. It doesn't work like that, either. Your soul doesn't say to another soul, "Sorry about that bullet in the brain at Fort Sumter, now how's about we meet up in Afghanistan and *you* take *me* out?"

So, if there's no punishment, and you don't agree to be the victim after being the perpetrator, is there no justice? Well, of course, there is. Here's how karma works:

Certain behavior creates a karmic debt. That means you'll be required to reap what you sowed at some point in the future. To create a karmic debt, you must have compromised another soul's life plan in some way. For obvious reasons, murder pretty much tops the list. If you take someone's life, that person's life plan is over. But there are many other ways you can deliberately or inadvertently derail another person's life plan.

You may not have heard of Thomas Midgley Jr., but given the catastrophic and extremely karmic impact this unfortunate soul has had on the world, you should have!

As a chemist at General Motors in the early 1920s, Thomas Midgley discovered that introducing lead into car engines via gasoline made them run better. For the next fifty years, every vehicle ran on leaded gas. It wasn't until the early '70s that it was finally removed—even though the enormous health risks were a matter of public knowledge—and had been from the get go.

To avoid causing alarm, the lead in gasoline wasn't called that. Instead, Midgley used the technical term, tetra-ethyl.

Midgley used a press conference to show there was nothing

to worry about. He demonstrated its safety by pouring tetra ethyl all over his hands, even breathing in the vapors to make his point. What no one knew was that this public display of nonchalance resulted in Midgley secretly spending time in the hospital afterwards, suffering from lead poisoning.

Lead in gasoline harmed millions of people before it was eventually banned. Some researchers have suggested that the crime wave that peaked in the 1990s was the result of lead poisoning. From a spiritual point of view, Thomas Midgley's legacy is appalling.

But wait! It gets worse! Midgley also invented chlorofluorocarbons (CFCs), the refrigerants responsible for creating a hole in the ozone layer. The impact of CFCs on humanity may well exceed that of lead, due to long-term repercussions like increased skin cancers.

Later in life, Midgley contracted polio and became bedridden. He used his ingenuity to rig up a system of pulleys to maneuver himself in bed. One day he got all tangled up in his contraption and died of asphyxiation.

An environmental historian remarked that Midgley "had more impact on the atmosphere than any other single organism in Earth's history." Author Bill Bryson wrote that Midgley possessed "an instinct for the regrettable that was almost uncanny."

Thomas Midgley Jr. was responsible for thousands of deaths. Since he was aware of the dangers of lead in gasoline, there was an extra level of culpability. His soul will spend lifetimes atoning for the damage caused. It will look for ways to experience the "other side of the coin."

Everyone must have a soul. And some souls will be born as children affected by lead in the atmosphere. Midgley's soul will be one of them. It will feel impelled to see the obverse side of the coin.

In many future lives, the soul that once was Midgley will find ways to heal others and create a better world. It will choose to be a healer, an environmentalist, a social worker, and a volunteer.

Which raises an interesting question: Is every humanitarian or healer making up for bad stuff they did in an earlier life?

You heal a karmic debt by helping someone in the present who is being victimized or negatively affected by the kind of actions you once perpetrated.

You might volunteer with orphans because you once abandoned a child, or become a surgeon because you once killed a lot of people. My guides refer to this form of atonement as Spiritual Acts.

Because karma is about balance, without exploring your past lives, there's no real way to tell whether you were once the victim or the perpetrator. If you were a prisoner of conscience in a past life, you might, as the victim of injustice, be drawn to support Amnesty International now. That allows you to help those who suffer as you once did.

If you were the one who jailed people for their political beliefs, you might, as the perpetrator, balance the karma in exactly the same way as the victim.

Thomas Midgley's karmic debt is enormous, and he'll spend many incarnations balancing the consequences of causing so many deaths. What, though, of his death from asphyxiation, tangled up in the ropes and weights of his own invention? Was it some kind of karma? It might look that way, but it was just an unfortunate accident.

UNFINISHED BUSINESS

Neil called me for his first session with no questions whatsoever. All I had was his name. So I simply had my spirit guides acknowledge him and went with the first thing they gave me.

"You were involved in the development of the world's first

submarines," I said. "Your specialty was pitch, yaw, and roll. Does that mean anything to you?"

To say Neil was astonished would be an understatement. He said, "I think about pitch, yaw, and roll all the time! I'm always looking for ways to use them more effectively."

(I had to look this one up: Pitch, yaw, and roll are "the angles of rotation in three dimensions about the vehicle's center of mass," but I'm sure you knew that.)

An hour later, he sent me an email with links to videos of various devices he'd designed and constructed, like a flight simulator for his two kids. He included the sketch of a plan for something he was building, pointing out the three annotations that read, "pitch," "yaw," and "roll." In this case, a short, disappointing past life had left his soul wanting to complete a circle of exploration.

Neil is simply continuing the exploration that had obsessed him in another life. And that's something all of us are doing in some way or other.

IN A ROOM OF A HUNDRED PEOPLE...

You'll often see signs of unfinished business in children. I told Kimberly that her six-year old daughter, Emma, had been an orchestra conductor in a recent lifetime. "That explains it," Kimberley said. "When we asked her what she wanted for her birthday, she said, 'I want a conductor's baton.'"

Put a hundred six-year-olds in a room and ask them what they want for their birthdays. I bet Emma would be the only one asking for a conductor's baton.

SPIRITUAL HOMES

For karmic reasons, you might find yourself drawn to places that have happy memories for your soul. Conversely, you may get a strangely uncomfortable feeling visiting a place where you once died horribly.

After seeing a particularly gruesome death in one client's past life, I suggested she'd be in no hurry to visit France. She told me that she'd travelled all through Europe on a rail card when she was a student.

She loved the whole experience—except for France. She crossed the border and left after one hour!

Another one of my clients also had a dreadful death in France. When I asked her if she'd ever visited the country she said, "I tried it three times. I just couldn't do it."

And when I warned one client that the past life I was starting to uncover involved domestic violence in Ireland, she exclaimed, "Ugh! I'm allergic to Ireland."

On the other hand, when I told Louise that she'd had the "best life ever" as a restaurant owner in Amalfi, Italy, she said, "I went there once. I felt I was home!"

She also loves to cook in this life, which is a karmic resonance from the past. "Feeding people feeds my soul," she said.

Since I was soon to be visiting Italy on my honeymoon, I was curious about her impression of other parts of Italy.

"Was there anywhere else you'd recommend?" I asked.

"Oh, I only went to Amalfi," she said.

And that spoke volumes about how strongly her soul was drawn to reconnect with that particular location where she'd once been so happy.

For some people, the desire to revisit a spiritual home is so compelling that they'll relocate to that place permanently. For others, a long weekend might be enough to get a taste of it again.

IN A ROOM OF A HUNDRED PEOPLE...

The resonances from happy past lives frequently show up in future lifetimes in unusual ways. When I spoke to Sherri in her home in South Africa, I found that her happiest moments from a life in England during the early 1900s were playing cricket with her grandfather.

I said, "Before I tell you about this life, I want to ask you a question. Do you like playing cricket?"

She said, "I love cricket! Especially batting!"

I pointed out that if I put her in a room with a hundred people, I'd expect her to be the only one to have such an enthusiastic response to my question.

BALANCING ACTS

Rachel was once a young boy enslaved in the American South during the 1800s, who lost his sight due to a parasitic disease. His blindness caused him to have a serious accident, and he developed septicemia. He died alone while his parents were laboring in the fields.

Rachel found the mention of septicemia particularly illuminating. "The first time I heard about it as a child, I had an enormous fear of it. When my brother and I were little, he accidentally stepped on an old metal coffee can filled with nails and sliced his foot open.

"Even though he was the one who was injured, I probably cried louder than he did because I was sure it was going to get infected and he'd die. Thankfully, my dad, who was a doctor, stitched him up, put a bandage on it, and before you know it we were playing again."

Not surprisingly, Rachel also has a huge fear of blindness and imprisonment in this life. But it's her career choice that's the most significant result of this sad past life.

To karmically balance the lessons from having been a sick and disempowered child, she became a healer specializing in trauma and accidents. As she put it, "I sometimes feel that my career chose me more than I chose it."

Like a lot of healers, Rachel's career began more through necessity than choice. "When my husband had an extraordinary 'spontaneous' remission from a rare blood disease, I became fascinated with how people heal," she said.

"I thought everyone should know the power of using imagery and how healing limiting beliefs and past traumas seemed to be at the core of so much of our disease processes. I was also very curious about ancient healing methods, as well as how Western medicine developed and became what it is today.

"I've specialized in working with chronic health challenges, especially anything with inflammation rather than acute medical problems. I chose that mostly because I started working with clients who had cancer or chronic pain. I'd healed myself from chronic pain. Now I do work with clients who have been in accidents and are dealing with chronic pain or the effects of trauma."

GOOD KARMA

Rachel has devoted her life to healing others and has helped me out a couple of times. So I was delighted to return the favor when she asked me if I could do anything about her high blood pressure.

I used a simple visualization technique to bring it back to

normal. And, as she told me later, "It's been good since the moment I got off the phone with you, and it's remained that way."

That's karma!

CREATIVE LIVES

During our first session together, the spirit guides told Dana her life purpose could be summed up in three words: creativity, creativity, and creativity.

Several past lives have contributed to her creativity now. In her first session with me, I told her that in the 1800s, as a jeweler for the Romanovs, Russia's royal family, she'd made intricate silver pieces that still exist in the Hermitage Museum in St. Petersburg.

When Dana said, "I spend hours at a time on the Hermitage online," I joked that she was looking for her own work—then it struck me that she was, quite unconsciously, doing just that.

In a later session, we uncovered a creative past life that could be easily researched. The spirit guides said, "She was a famous landscape painter in Norfolk, England—the artist John Crome."

Dana, it turned out, has always had a fascination with the Regency period in England, which coincides with the time she was there.

In this life, Dana has the opportunity to become well known and must (the spirit guides were insistent) exhibit her work. A few months later, when I asked how things were going, she was preparing for a show.

"Recently," she said, "I've been exploring landscapes and portraiture through photography. As for the spirit guides' advice, I'm planning a black and white portrait project in the fall."

IN A ROOM OF A HUNDRED PEOPLE...

Dana has had many lives (including this one) as an artist, the most recent one being as a male sculptor in Paris. Unfortunately, in that particular life, the artist lost his entire studio and all his work to creditors after being stiffed by a client.

As a result of this experience, she stockpiles art supplies and buys lots of similar materials so she always has a choice. When she took up photography, she bought not one, but four cameras.

But after the past-life work we did kicked in she told me, "My need to keep acquiring cameras has eased. I'm also feeling it's time to thin out my other stockpiles and clear psychic space for making art. What a relief!"

In a room of a hundred people, I imagine no one else would be so concerned about losing the contents of their studio that they bought duplicates of everything "just in case."

THE NEED FOR EMPOWERMENT

In many ways, balancing karma keeps the world turning. The desire to help those who suffer now as you once did is the reason so many old souls get involved in charitable or volunteer work.

Monique had a past life in which she was shipped from Africa to become enslaved in Mississippi. She suffered terribly from being anally raped and died young as a result of appendicitis and septicemia.

"I imagine this past life resonates in a lot of ways," I said. "I'd expect an Achilles body part, a weakness, in your anus or that general area."

Monique recognized the resonance immediately. "I had a blood clot in my colon from birth control pills," she said. "It caused me to hemorrhage painfully."

When I told her she could heal from this past-life trauma by helping women dealing with the effects of rape, she was already there.

"I recently became part of a committee helping victims of sexual violence," she said. "And, just yesterday, we had a meeting about human trafficking."

Like many of the people I work with, Monique had followed her soul's guidance and was finding ways to balance karma from the past. And like most of them, she was quite unaware of the source of the motivation to help others.

I've found, however, that once most people become conscious of why their soul wants to balance karma, the validation empowers them and encourages them to do more.

THE WIND IN YOUR HAIR

My client's 19-year old daughter, Laura, had a past life as a political prisoner and died serving a life sentence on a remote island in the Pacific (the kind of mosquito-infested nightmare location featured in the movie "Papillon").

Laura's soul is urging her to balance the karma. When she finishes college, she plans to work in the prison system.

After lives of restraint, souls will seek ways to balance the experience through activities that give them a sense of freedom and the feeling of "wind in their hair."

The most common karmic signs are riding horses or motorcycles, cycling, surfing, skiing, and driving convertibles.

When I asked her mother if Laura rode horses, the answer was, "Fast!"

Having suffered terrible injustice in a previous life, many old souls balance the karma by making the world a fairer place. And like anyone whose life-plan has been derailed by false accusations, Lesley has strong feelings around justice and fairness.

Her past life in Russia became derailed when she was falsely accused of theft and jailed for five years. When she was released, the country was in chaos due to the 1917 Revolution. She discovered that her children had been taken into care, but could never find out where.

To balance the karma from that life, Lesley is heavily involved with a nonprofit organization that helps girls in Morocco to stay in school. When I first spoke to her, they'd recently been visited by former First Lady Michelle Obama and the actress Meryl Streep.

"These girls had no place to study or do art projects after school," Lesley told me. "We've provided opportunities they would never have otherwise had."

When a soul has been disempowered in a past life (and imprisonment and slavery are the ultimate forms of disempowerment), the key to personal healing is to empower others.

LEAVING A LEGACY

Many old souls have a desire for Immortality. In fact, you're probably one of them. Does it mean you want to live forever? No, but it means you want to do something that lasts beyond your time here.

The desire for Immortality is part of your soul's life plan, and like everything else in your life plan, you chose it before you were even born. It impels you to help others and to find effective ways to balance karma.

Having a desire for Immortality is about leaving a legacy, creating a ripple effect, or doing something that helps others fulfill their own life plan. Despite its grand title, a desire for Immortality doesn't mean you have to change the world.

Martin Luther King Jr. had it. Mother Teresa, too. But so do many nurses, caregivers, and healers. One of my clients expresses her desire for Immortality by helping poor immigrants find housing.

There are many reasons an old soul will want to help others. It can be the result of your soul type, your missions, karma, or simply old-soul altruism. The difference is that a desire for Immortality involves a long-term view of things.

Your soul wants the ripple effect to keep spreading, and that can mean the difference between giving someone the proverbial fish and teaching them how to do it for themselves. And sometimes it involves giving voice to those who can't speak for themselves.

Carrie is an academic. I knew she wrote books, and we'd joked about how having the Performer soul type in her personality meant she wouldn't always be happy writing books, only for them to end up sitting on a shelf in a college library being checked out once every ten years. She needed an audience.

But when it came to her second session with me, it was clear that her desire for Immortality was the real driving force behind her need to reach a wider audience.

I found a past life in Spain in which Carrie had been a picador, the bullfighter on horseback who tortures the bull by repeatedly stabbing it in the back of the neck. Finding that her day job in that life was as a butcher, I was prompted to ask, "Are you a vegetarian?"

"I became a vegetarian when I was eighteen," she said.

There's usually no karma associated with being a butcher

unless you inflicted unnecessary cruelty on an animal. But being a bullfighter is another matter. I started telling Carrie that she might want to consider addressing the karma by working for animal rights.

Sometimes when I pick up information from my spirit guides, the tense is not clear. A person may be guided to do something, or they're already doing it. Carrie was already taking care of karmic business. "That's what I do," she said. "My work is all about ethics and animal rights.

And it was the topic of spirit guides that came up next. "Who are my spirit guides?" Carrie asked.

It turned out one of them was (two lifetimes ago) the Scottish author Gavin Maxwell, who wrote the book *Ring of Bright Water* about an otter named Tarka.

The soul that was once Maxwell is completing its own karma by helping several animal writers now. Though Maxwell's book was a huge success, and even made into a film, his soul feels that mental illness prevented him from achieving more in that life.

Carrie had another question. "Is that why I called my son Gavin? She asked.

"Great question," I said. I asked my spirit guides, "Is Carrie's decision to name her son Gavin more than just coincidence?" My spirit guides have a sense of humor that can border on sarcasm when I ask the obvious.

"What do you think?" they replied, implying that some things really are, as they're fond of saying, not rocket science.

Like Carrie, many old souls fulfill their desire for Immortality by writing books. But there are many other ways. Some do it by recording music. An architect might build an apartment block. A painter with a desire for Immortality hopes her work will find a permanent spot on someone's wall.

And when our time on this planet comes to an end, and cock-roaches rule the world, what will alien archeologists find?

Pottery. Talk about creating something that lasts beyond your time here.

Your own desire for Immortality can be played out in any number of ways. The most common sign that you have it is an underlying desire (hence the title) to help improve, elevate, inspire, or better the lives of others. It's all about raising your consciousness while simultaneously balancing any karmic debts you might owe from prior incarnations.

KINDNESS AND KARMA

As an old soul, it's unlikely you'll want to live indefinitely. (By the time they reach Level 10, most souls have been around the block so often that they're quite eager to get back to the comfort of the Astral Plane.)

But you may well have that underlying urge to do something that will allow you to eventually look back on this life and say, "I left the world a little better than I found it."

At its core, your soul is not arrogant. It doesn't give two hoots about proving it's right. It doesn't get jealous or mistrustful. It values knowledge and understanding. It decries hypocrisy, shuns callous indifference, and never tries to control others. Your soul is fundamentally kind.

Unfortunately, your soul takes a real beating as it makes its way through its many incarnations here on Planet Earth. As we've seen, the karmic consequences of Physical Plane trauma cause the soul to carry fears, blocks, and limiting beliefs with it on its journey.

If you had a past life in which you were unkind to another human being by abusing your authority, your soul will carry the memory into this life. It will endeavor to balance the karma by supporting the underdog and generally offering kindness to less fortunate souls.

If you exploited others in a past life, your soul will be motivated to give this time around.

And even if you were the victim rather than perpetrator, the same principle applies. If your soul suffered abuse in an earlier life, it will balance the karma through caring and nurture.

Your soul will always push from behind the scenes in an effort to keep you doing what's right. When you suffer injustice, it will urge you to seek greater justice for yourself and others and avoid slipping into a fear-based thirst for vengeance.

Kindness is, in itself, karmic. The more kindness you bring into the world, the more you'll benefit in this life and the next. Hold a door open for someone, give them a smile, and feel the warmth emanate from their heart to yours.

On a more cosmic level, what you sow in this life, you'll reap in the next. We all know certain individuals who seem to have an inner sense of contentment. These are people whose souls have a deeper level of peace as a result of the kindness they brought into the world. They benefit from the karmic consequences of spirituality.

You can make a considerable impression on other souls in this life and the next through simple acts of kindness. By acting spiritually, your influence can transform the lives of other souls and pave your way for a happier and more contented incarnation in the future.

EXERCISE: CREATING A RIPPLE EFFECT

Remember, you don't have to be Mother Teresa to leave a legacy and balance karma. The important thing is to do something, rather than nothing.

Take a pen and paper and make a list of things you could be doing right now to create a ripple effect, leave some kind of a legacy, or help others to live a better life. Then circle one of those things and take the necessary steps to begin doing it. Simple!

———

Kindness is an expression of love, and love is the ultimate goal of every soul. If you find yourself wondering how to accelerate your spiritual growth, the most effective way is through acts of kindness.

Most souls need love, as my spirit guides frequently point out, like fish need water. From life number one until now, your soul has been seeking out members of its soul family. It's with these particular souls that it can achieve the deepest intimacy.

But what about soulmates? What are they, and does everyone have one?

III

A LIFE WELL LIVED

9

SOULMATES AND OLD FRIENDS

THE SEARCH FOR CONNECTION

I firmly believe that if we better understood the whole subject of soulmates, it would change the way we approach our intimate relationships. Like almost everyone else on the planet, your soul is seeking love. Love is, after all, the ultimate goal to which it aspires. You may find it through friendships or the kind of connection you get with a parent, child, or a sibling. The deepest connection, however, is always reached through a loving relationship with an "old friend," a soul you've known in previous lifetimes.

Not only will you have shared past lives with an old friend, but you'll both be from the same soul family, the group of souls who started their Physical Plane journey at the same time, many thousands of years ago.

While you may have been married to an old friend in a past life, not all old friends you encounter in this life are meant to be romantic relationships. Though the spirit guides will use the word "soulmate" to indicate a particularly close friendship, they generally use the term to describe an old friend with whom you have a romantic agreement.

Does everyone have a soulmate? Of the thousands of people

I've worked with, I've met only two who have no need for a relationship. It shows up in their life plan as a mission of Avoidance, with absolutely no mission of Connection. (Missions are part of your life plan and something I go into more detail about in *The Instruction*). For these two clients, being in a relationship would be incredibly stressful. They live alone and are happy with their own company. Their isolation is part of their life plan, not the result of any fear.

Everyone else I've ever worked with is either in a relationship or seeking one, with a soulmate connection being the ideal. And if they say, "I don't need one," they're whistling in the dark, pretending they're doing okay despite not having the love their soul truly needs.

A person who scoffs at the idea of there even being such a thing as a soulmate is much more likely to end up in a second-rate relationship. They might choose a partner based on looks, money, or social status. The person who understands the importance of finding their soulmate is searching for something much deeper.

Have you ever met someone and felt you've known them before? You can usually recognize a soulmate by that sense of familiarity. The moment you encounter them, your soul will try to alert you. It will want you to know that this is somebody who's special and who could become an important part of your life.

Some people worry that they're not ever going to meet their soulmate or that somehow they'll miss that person. Around the time that I first began working with my spirit guides, they told me I had a soulmate on the way.

I said, "Great! But I'm planning a trip to Hawaii. Should I cancel it and stay here in California?"

"What if she's in Hawaii?"

"Is she?"

They said the last thing they wanted me to do was alter any plans. I just had to be open to meeting her. I didn't have to be at the corner of Hyde and Sacramento in two days' time, or on a beach in Maui at 9:17 a.m. on a particular morning.

The universe goes to enormous lengths to make sure that we connect with one another. It's the great game, if you like. It's what the spirit guides are doing all the time—helping us to connect and form a relationship.

Fortunately, we have more than one soulmate agreement. Some of them we'll use and some of them we won't. It's like if you miss a bus or something happens to prevent you from getting on that bus. Another one will come along a little bit later.

Souls make agreements with one another on the Astral Plane all the time. The purpose is to make sure that if you're meant to be in a relationship, it will happen. But if you fail to connect with one person, your soul will recalibrate. It will have other agreements. And they're never fallback positions. They're never lesser. They're just different.

Agreements created on the Astral Plane don't always work out as anticipated once you get here. The one I'd been waiting for didn't, in fact. After we split up, I used to joke, "We had 12 great years. Then we met."

We went our separate ways by choice. Sadly, some soulmate agreements come to a catastrophic and premature end, and it's no one's choice.

LOSING A SOULMATE

No matter how carefully you plan your life before each incarnation, things will still go wrong. The loss of a soulmate is, unfortunately, not uncommon. The spiritual and emotional effects of such a loss can be debilitating and causes some individuals to isolate themselves to avoid the risk of further loss.

During my first session with Alexia, I told her to expect her soulmate to come along very soon. By the next time we spoke, she'd met him. His name was David, and he was a soldier with the U.S. Army. Sadly, they only had the chance to spend a short time together before he had to redeploy to Afghanistan.

"We weren't just in love," Alexia said, "We were crazy in love!" For almost a month, they talked regularly via Skype. Then one evening he didn't check in. He and other members of his unit had been killed by a bomb while on patrol earlier that day. "I was totally devastated," she said.

When two soulmates lose each other so prematurely, both souls (even if one is on the Astral Plane) will feel a sense of unfinished business. They'll pine for each other. They'll want to reconnect.

Souls who are on the Astral Plane are usually more motivated to make contact with those of us who are still incarnate than the other way around. In part, it's because they have a greater awareness of the potential for communication.

It only took a day or two for David to make his presence known. "He came to me in a dream," Alexia said, "And he handed me a peacock feather. When I woke up I thought, 'What the heck does that mean?' But when I discovered that a peacock feather represents eternal life, I got it!"

And then, a few days later, something out of the ordinary happened. Alexia's aunt was visiting to help comfort her. In the middle of the night they were both startled by the sound of music from another room. "I had one of those old-fashioned answering machines," Alexia said. "It was playing *If I Could Build My World Around You* by Marvin Gaye. We knew it was David's way of getting in touch.

"We pressed the button and it played the song again. And each time we played it, the sound faded. By morning there was nothing—no sign of a message or music anywhere."

For over a year, David would cause the lights to flicker, and Alexia could even feel him touch her. But over time, the visits became less frequent.

"Sometimes I'd ask him if he was still there and the lights

would flicker," Alexia said. "But I felt I needed to start letting him go. Then Mike, one of the guys in his unit, appeared to me in a dream. I told him I wasn't a medium, but he kept pointing to his throat. I knew it was a message for his wife.

"Soon after, there was a memorial for families of the soldiers who'd been killed on active duty. As soon as I saw Mike's wife, I knew why he kept pointing at his throat. She was wearing his ring on a chain around her neck. I went up to her and said, 'He knows you wear his ring.' She was blown away. She said, 'I've been praying for a sign. Thank you!'"

If you have a soul connection with someone, it means you'll have a connection with people in their world too. Alexia didn't meet David's mother until the funeral, but immediately became part of the family. Alexia described what happened on what would have been David's birthday.

"It was the night before his birthday. He came to me again in a dream. This time he said he wanted to put his energy into seeing his mom. It was distressing to her that she'd never seen him in the year since he passed. But at 6:00 a.m., she called me and said, 'I saw him in a dream—and I know you had something to do with it!'"

Recently, David's mother had a question for Alexia. She asked, "If you'd known what would happen, would you still have gone for it?" Alexia didn't have to think. "In a heartbeat," she replied. "And I'd do it again."

Alexia sees what happened as something profoundly spiritual. "I hear the voice of a higher power through his voice. I learned that when we pass, we all go back to the source. He passed while he was in love. And we still love each other very much. We truly gave each other the gift of love."

When I last spoke to Alexia, I asked if she'd met anyone else. "It's been five years," she said, "I haven't met anyone, but it's okay. I feel complete."

We both agreed that Alfred, Lord Tennyson had it right when

he wrote in his poem *In Memoriam*, "'Tis better to have loved and lost than never to have loved at all."

It might interest you to know that the original title of that poem was "The Way of the Soul."

MAYA ANGELOU

When you meet a soulmate, you should know it. Most often, you'll feel that still, small voice of your soul telling you, "This could be the one!" Conversely, when someone is not right for you, your soul will tug at your sleeve to let you know something is amiss.

The key is to step back a little and check in quietly to see what kind of message you're getting.

Of course, getting into a relationship can cause the most level headed amongst us to throw caution to the wind and ignore the red flags and sirens that our souls and spirit guides are using to get our attention.

You can be drawn strongly to someone because they're from your soul family. That's good. You want that. And you can be drawn to someone because you have shared lessons to learn. Again, that will be supported.

But you can also find yourself sucked into a toxic relationship because of patterns that you have yet to consciously recognize. And if you see any kind of pattern emerging when you scan your relationships, the chances are that you're doing this. I've worked with clients who've spent their lives drawn to "bad boys," alcoholics, emotionally or geographically unavailable partners, or all different kinds of users, losers, or abusers.

And I've worked with clients who've met a soulmate but it hasn't worked out. Just because someone's an old friend, they can still be a jerk. While all souls are inherently loving, sometimes experiences on the Physical Plane can cause a person to act unkindly. When it comes to a romantic agreement between two souls, there is no obligation to keep plugging away when things are obviously not working out.

People change. The person you are now is very different from who you were twenty years ago. And this principle applies to relationships, too. A relationship can morph and change, and it's not always for the better.

In my experience, a soul-level agreement most commonly fails to take root because of the effects of fear, alcohol abuse, or some kind of personality disorder. What looks like the perfect plan when your souls made the agreement on the Astral Plane can look very different when you actually meet.

When I first spoke to Susan, she was going through divorce after five years in a destructive marriage. The problem was his drinking.

"On our first date, we drained two bottles of wine in an hour. And he drank most of it," she told me.

And that's when my spirit guides first uttered the words, "Maya Angelou."

When I work with my spirit guides, we encounter a lot of issues and questions that come up regularly, so they use shorthand to help speed things up.

In this case, instead of them telling me something like, "This person saw all the warning signs early in the relationship, but refused to acknowledge them," they simply said, "Maya Angelou."

It was a reference to a quote from the esteemed poet who said, "When someone shows you who they are, believe them the first time."

If that statement resonates with you, I urge you to print it out and keep it in plain sight to act as a reminder that souls are compelled to reveal themselves—for good or bad—in the early days, weeks, or months of a relationship. The problem is not that we don't see who people are, but that we choose to ignore the red flags.

Even the most compelling relationship should not be entered

into without some discernment. All the signs to look out for will show up very early on. Sometimes even on the first date. If they get hammered, insult the wait staff, turn up an hour late, or say, "My relationship with my ex? It's complicated..." then don't be surprised if problems pop up sometime in the future.

Your soul's desire to reconnect with a soul family member can blind you to problems that may be significant. An abuser may have a history that causes alarm, yet convince you that somehow your presence has made them a different person. Or someone might say, "Yes, I cheated on all those others, but of course I'd never do that to you."

Souls carry with them a strong level of idealism. Unfortunately, it can push you to choose a fixer-upper in the belief that you can somehow turn that person into your ideal with just a little elbow grease and a new coat of paint.

When you follow the guidance of both heart and mind, and are careful not to override your intuition, you set yourself up for success. And remember that when someone shows you who they are, you'll see the good as well as the bad. If they turn up at the stroke of eight, love their mother, are kind to dogs and cats (or whatever else you see as a virtue), then pay attention to that, too.

And remember that when someone says, "I've had an epiphany, and I'm no longer the person I used to be," they may well be right. The past is not always prologue, even if previous behavior can so often be a predictor of future behavior.

The only way to truly be certain, without giving it 20 years or hiring a private detective to follow them around, is to be aware of the voice of your soul and pay attention to what it tells you. Recognize that the best decisions are those made using discernment that is both intellectual and intuitive.

TRUST ISSUES

Let's say you're in a relationship. Maybe everything's fine and there's no cause for worry, but you just can't seem to trust your partner. You might worry that they won't be there when you need them or that they're up to something behind your back.

Or maybe you're with someone who doesn't trust you. They check up on you, interrogate you when you're a few minutes late, blame you for not being supportive, or even accuse you of having an affair.

If you're struggling with mistrust in your relationship, chances are the underlying cause is a past-life fear of Betrayal. Of course, if your partner has cheated on you in this life, your fear will be perfectly rational. But in the absence of any specific reason for mistrust, the cause is usually from prior incarnations.

One of my clients had a past life as a woman in Italy back in the early 1800s. Her husband cheated on her from the moment they were married, stole her money, and then dumped her. In this life, she's married to a great guy who loves her dearly and would never dream of having an affair. Yet she couldn't help obsessing that he would. "One time, I accused him of having a thing for my cousin," she said, "even though they only met once when we got married and she lives in another state. I think I'm paranoid!"

She wasn't paranoid. She was simply suffering from a past-life fear of Betrayal that was triggered in this lifetime by getting married. Her soul worried that history would repeat itself. All we needed to do to ease the fear was to remind her soul that what happened in Italy was "then" and this is "now" and that the fear was inappropriate.

Many people can become quite irrational when they fear betrayal in a relationship. In a past life, they might have faced a betrayal of expectations in a court of law and ended up in prison. Or they could have suffered betrayal from a mother who abandoned them. The consequences in the past life might have been devastating.

Because the soul can't easily separate this life from ones that have gone before, it overreacts to what it perceives as a threat. Irrational behavior is the result.

To ease a past life fear of Betrayal, it's important to tell the difference between fear and reality. If your partner takes business trips where they never seem to get cell phone coverage, or can't account for their absence, or if they always take their phone to the bathroom with them, then you have every right to be suspicious.

But if they treat you respectfully, show up when expected, and have no track record of disloyalty, then you need to ask yourself if your mistrust is simply your fear of betrayal from a previous incarnation keeping you on high alert.

Conversely, if you're with someone who mistrusts you when you've done nothing, it can get pretty tiring having to put up with multiple calls when you're late coming home or when you have to treat someone with kid gloves to avoid triggering their accusations. If their previous partner in this lifetime cheated on them, you might find yourself coming under suspicion for little or no reason.

To ease the friction when mistrust is present in a relationship, it helps to be open with your fears. Discuss your concerns—whether you're the one with the fear or the one dealing with your partner's fear. Mistrust thrives on secrecy, so transparency is the quickest way to stop it from interfering with the harmony of your relationship.

If your partner is the one struggling with a past-life fear of betrayal, have patience with them. Gently help their soul come to the understanding that the past is the past and their fear is no longer relevant in this lifetime.

Every one of the past life fears can be triggered when two souls meet. Intimacy can be blocked through fear when one or both have past lives involving rape or sexual abuse. Losing a partner a hundred years ago can cause a person to push their loved ones away because they dread the thought of re-experiencing the devastating grief in this life.

THE WORST CASE SCENARIO

If you lost your current soulmate in an earlier incarnation, you might find yourself going to a dark place when they're late coming home and you can't get in touch. If your fear is truly significant, it goes something like this:

- One minute late: You check the time.
- Five minutes late: You worry there's been a terrible accident.
- Ten minutes late: You picture yourself rushing to the hospital
- Twenty minutes late: Tears well up as you visualize giving the eulogy at their funeral.

Many couples feel impelled to be together despite some big fears being triggered. The need to work on shared karmic lessons takes precedence over anything else. Like magnets constantly switching polarity, they attract and repel simultaneously.

If you've ever said, "I can't live with them, but can't live without them," you're describing a karmic relationship. You might be going through life with the person who abandoned you when things got tough in Sumatra 300 years ago. In which case, you might adore them, but always feel a little anger or mistrust towards them as well.

As one of my clients—someone whose husband cheated her out of a business in a previous life—put it, "We've been together 40 years and he drives me nuts. But I can't imagine life without him."

THE ANGEL PRINCIPLE

When my spirit guides describe someone as an angel, they're not referring to some kind of otherworldly being.

An earth angel is someone from your soul family who comes into your life to act as a catalyst for change. Very often, they're the rebound relationship. Sometimes they're in your world for a few days and other times they can become a life partner.

What I love about earth angels is that we all get to be one. An earth angel is just as likely to be you as it is to be someone else. Once you recognize what it means to be an earth angel, you'll be able to look back at times when you've been one.

I had a conversation about this once at Hollyhock Retreat Centre in Canada. I told a staff member there named Camille about the angel principle—how a certain person can come into your life as a catalyst—and she recognized it immediately."

A young man named Edward had visited the Centre for a workshop the previous summer. Shortly before my arrival, he made a return visit. He said to her, "What you told me when I was here last year changed my life."

Like a lot of people who act as earth angels, Camille only vaguely recalled what she might have said to effect such a trans-formation. She said to him, "I remember thinking it, but I never actually said it." But Edward was adamant. "What you said liter-ally changed my life!"

This example illustrates two fundamental aspects of the angel principal. The first is that you say something that helps the other person see things in a new way. The second is that the person who delivers the message often doesn't remember or has only a hazy recollection of having said something.

The reason the messenger so often can't recall saying anything of any significance is because, in that moment, they were channeling. Being a conduit for messages from spirit guides means that what was said doesn't always end up in your memory banks. (After one client told me, "You know what you've done for me!" I had to admit I hadn't a clue.)

For instance, Jeannie is a client who met a woman on a retreat. They hit it off immediately. This is a sign of soul connection and, in fact, I confirmed that they were both from the same soul family. I said they were acting as angels to one another.

"That explains it," she said. "My friend is a writer, and she told me she was going to change a whole chapter of her book based on something I suggested." I have absolutely no recollection of having that conversation."

An earth angel might be the friend you meet some time before ending a major relationship. They could be a therapist or a psychic. Whatever shape or form they take, their purpose is to get you out of a rut, inspire much needed change, or to show you how much better your life can be.

The message you get from an earth angel is the voice of your spirit guides. The guides use earth angels to communicate when you're unable or unwilling to hear them any other way. And you, as an old soul, will be an earth angel to others more than once on your journey through this life.

SEXUAL DYSFUNCTION

From a spiritual point of view, great sex is up there with meditation, yoga, and chocolate. It may not be essential, but it can radically enhance your enjoyment of life on earth.

As I mentioned earlier, because your soul is unable to separate mind, body, and spirit, if one part of the trio is blocked, it will affect the other two. This is why illness can lead to depression, depression can lead to illness, and lousy sex can make you miserable.

There are many reasons for sexual problems and the most common—yet the one few people would ever think of—is trauma from past lives. Sadly, many individuals and couples struggle with problems that can be relatively easily dealt with through past-life exploration.

PHYSICAL MEMORIES OF SEXUAL TRAUMA

Linda had a devastating experience in an earlier incarnation, in which she was violently raped and assaulted by American soldiers stationed in Manila. I told her that her soul associates sex with death, and how sexual trauma often shows up in future lives as fibroids or ovarian cysts.

"I had a twenty-pound ovarian cyst removed," she said. "There was no explanation."

"This past life must have caused a lot of problems in your relationships," I suggested.

"I don't know," she replied, "I'm 40, but I've never had one."

I told Jeff about a past life in Spain in which, as a boy, he'd been abused by a priest. In that life, he'd developed a huge amount of shame around sex, particularly ejaculation.

Well, it turned out that Jeff had been struggling with the effects of this past life for as long as he could remember. The resonance from the abuse he'd once suffered caused immense stress around sex. "I've never been able to get—or keep—an erection," he told me.

When he called for his second session, to say Jeff was ecstatic about the shifts he'd experienced since we first spoke would have been an understatement.

"I'm amazed!" he said. "What you did was stunning! Everything changed immediately. I'm almost 60 and I've had this problem since I was a kid. Overnight, I became completely functional."

I said, "I'm always thrilled when someone tells me they've healed 20 years of…"

"20 years?" he said. "Try 40 or more! I'm totally speechless!"

I was reminded of something my spirit guides will often say: "You can't have great sex on the Astral Plane." In other words, you're here to learn what it is to be human, and sex is an essential part of the lesson.

THE SPIRITUAL VIEW OF SEX

During a Q&A session in my Soul World membership program, I was asked, "I have a past life or two as a courtesan, or high paid prostitute. In this life, I'm still confused about men and money and the power dynamic between men and women. What effects can linger in a soul, after a life or lives as a prostitute?"

There's no simple answer to this question. Some past-life occupations have resonances you might expect. Ancient mariners like messing around on boats in this life. Medieval jewelers are drawn to gemstones and jewelry now.

But being a prostitute in a past life doesn't show up in any one way. It all depends on the culture and the experiences. If someone became a prostitute because they were forced into it, in this life they'll react with an emphatic, "Don't tell me what to do!" if they so much as smell coercion.

Many sex workers are attracted to a career that offers

personal freedom, flexible hours, and the opportunity to provide an essential service, particularly after a past life in which they had none of those things.

And some are drawn to the business in the same way a person who was a professor in a past life will gravitate towards academia. It's a world that feels familiar to them.

If sex in a past life was nothing more than a physical act, then this life will be all about seeking intimate connection. A client who'd been forced into prostitution a century ago told me how she couldn't imagine having sex without an emotional connection.

HEALING THE EFFECTS OF SEXUAL VIOLENCE

Katrina was having some major relationship problems stemming from her rape in both this and a past life. She'd shut down sexually and her husband was sympathetic, but also suffering greatly. We found the source of the original (past life) trauma, and I told her we'd see how things were going the next time we spoke.

A few months later, she called for her next session, and before I could even say hello, she said, "My husband thinks you're amazing!"

All souls are meant to enjoy sex. It's not just about procreation or letting off steam. It's a way to build intimacy between souls. Sex is intended to be empowering and is a way many past-life prostitutes, or victims of sexual abuse and rape, can take back their power.

What about polygamy or polyamory? What's the spiritual take

on having more than one spouse or lover? Unless deceit is involved, there's no judgment.

With very few exceptions, however, all souls are seeking intimacy, and having multiple partners at the same time blocks the ability to reach the deepest level of connection.

Souls are essentially monogamous and don't want to split the energy associated with intimacy by trying to achieve it with more than one other soul at a time. This doesn't mean having multiple partners simultaneously is right or wrong. It's simply a choice. It's just not the soul's choice. It can also be a convenient way to avoid facing real intimacy.

When it comes to what's appropriate or not, I've found the spirit guides to be remarkably broad minded. Role playing, they say, can be a way to safely regain lost power or build trust. And ritual can connect lovers by turning a purely physical act into something more spiritual.

As long as sex is consensual, almost anything goes. For obvious reasons, sex with minors or anyone who is unable to freely consent to having sex is unacceptable.

Unfortunately, coercion is everywhere. If a powerful business man uses his position to take advantage of a lowly member of staff by threatening dismissal, then we all recognize the abuse. But the spirit guides see abuse where we on the Physical Plane often don't.

YOU'RE NEVER TOO OLD

I'm reminded of the time when my oldest son told me that he and other seniors were going to be teaching sex-ed at the middle school. My youngest came in at the tail end of the conversation and said, "Seniors teaching sex-ed? What do old people know about sex?"

My answer was, "A lot more than you think!" And it reminded me, too, of something the writer Robert Heinlein once said: "Each generation thinks it invented sex."

———————

Sex should never be used as a weapon. And from the perspective of the spirit guides, anything other than an enthusiastic "yes" means "no." If one partner threatens to withhold love to manipulate the other, that's abusive. If they bribe, cajole, or lie to get laid, that's abuse. Infidelity is never okay, since it involves deceit. Sex should be fun, and if one of the participants is not having fun, then the solution is to stop and figure it out.

Not everyone has a partner, or the opportunity for a healthy sex life. But whenever possible, the spirit guides will encourage my clients to work on it, even if it means a bit of DIY. The problem is that because the soul can't separate mind, body, and spirit, an absence of physical sensuality can negatively affect you spiritually and mentally, too.

So you can't have great sex on the Astral Plane, but neither can you have hugs and cuddles, or any of the other great things that come with a functional romantic relationship. Most souls, whether or not they know it, are on a search for physical, emotional, and spiritual intimacy.

———————

EXERCISE: FINDING A SOULMATE

If you're in the market for a soulmate, this exercise is for you. But even if you're not, I encourage you to try this exercise, because the simple principles apply to anything you want to manifest in this life.

- If you're looking for a relationship, list 20 things you want in your soulmate. Don't be afraid to ask for what you really want. Just because intimacy has been hard to find in the past, don't be afraid to put it on the list. Put your requests in a positive way. Use terms like "emotionally available" rather than "not still married."
- If you're currently in a relationship, and you feel there's room for improvement, list 20 things you want to change.
- And finally, if you're looking to create positive shifts in your life, take this opportunity to focus on 20 things you want to have happen.
- Once you've made your list, read it out loud to your spirit guides every day. Find a quiet place and say, "I call upon my spirit guides, acting in my highest interest…" Then read through the list to let them know what you want to bring into your life. Their job is to help you manifest the things you want. Give them the best chance to do so.

Now, let's take a look at soulmates of a different kind: children. Whether or not you have children, this next chapter will speak to you for the simple reason that you've been one yourself. And, as an old soul, that part of the journey might well have been the most challenging of all.

10

AN OLD SOUL IN A YOUNG BODY

NAVIGATING THE CHALLENGES OF CHILDHOOD

*A*s a sensitive old soul, you have as much chance of getting through childhood physically and emotionally unscathed as does a kangaroo in a minefield. The problem is not simply that you're easily damaged by the rough and tumble of life. It's that it can take little more than a sideways glance from a parent to trigger a past-life fear of Rejection, or a reprimand from a teacher to bring a past-life fear of Judgment or Inferiority rushing to the surface.

Violence, anger, and rage in childhood can leave lasting damage and plenty to explore on the analyst's couch when you grow up. The problem is that regular therapy doesn't deal with the source as much as the symptom. Remember, present life experiences act as a trigger for trauma from your soul's past. And as we've seen already, the deepest healing happens when the past-life causes are uncovered.

I want to share an experience from my own childhood. My reason for telling you this is because I healed decades of PTSD and other challenges stemming from the event. If I can do it, so can you. And you should, because you're worth the effort!

I'm the adult child of an alcoholic parent. And, of course, that means I was once simply the child of an alcoholic parent. Growing up in Scotland, I'm sure my family looked quite normal from the outside. But with a narcissistic, alcoholic father with anger issues and a mother who made it her mission to keep up appearances, things were far from what they seemed.

When I was eight years old, my father came into my bedroom one night when I was sick, held me upside down by my ankles and beat the crap out of me. Snot and tears were flying everywhere. My younger brother was screaming. I was screaming. My father finally threw me down and left me wailing hysterically. Then, a few minutes later, he came back into my room and started all over again. I thought he was going to kill me. Nothing was ever said in the family about what happened. I recall my mother's horror the next day when she saw the bruises on my body. I had to stay off school until the marks began to fade.

The familial dysfunction continued. My father had a mistress and numerous affairs, and he would disappear for days at a time. His rages were unpredictable. He could blow with little or no warning. During one of his drinking binges, things got so bad that my mother locked herself in the bathroom and slashed her wrists.

My mother, my brother, and I survived, but not without the chaos leaving a mark. The three of us were not embittered by our experiences—my mother was a compassionate and loving lady—and my brother is one of the most warm-hearted and generous people it's been my good fortune to know.

But my PTSD stemmed directly from the violence of my father, and my relationship choices in this life were shaped by the events of my childhood. Until I met my current wife, Christine, every long-term relationship I had was with someone who was either alcoholic, mentally ill, narcissistic, or all three.

No one wants to be a victim, but sometimes we just are. We become the victims of others' behavior and victims of the patterns we adopt without even being aware.

As a child, I became the placater, desperate to keep everything calm for fear of what might happen if things got out of control. As a teenager, my role became that of my mother's protector. I covered for my dad and worked with my mother to preserve the illusion of normalcy. And in my relationships as an adult I became the ultimate enabler, covering up, cleaning up endless messes, and sacrificing my own needs to accommodate theirs.

With a past-life fear of Inferiority (the result of an incarnation in which I was treated as worthless), my childhood experience (the trigger) trapped me in a place of submission; a giver who attracted takers. (Unconsciously, perpetrators seek out victims and vice versa.) Significantly, no one needs to make themselves feel superior at another's expense unless they, too, have this fear.)

But if I'd been carrying a strong past-life fear of Betrayal, it would have shown up as mistrust. And if my past-life fear had been one of Intimacy, I'd have struggled in this life with feeling safe enough to show my vulnerability.

Many of us are victimized by the events of our childhood. But there's a big difference between being a victim and being helpless. And, a little later in the book, I'll show you how to shift to a place of empowerment regardless of what kind of trauma you're carrying from childhood. The answer is to go to the past-life source and not only deal with the present-life symptoms.

First, I want to share a few stories to illustrate the healing potential of past-life work when it comes to dealing with childhood challenges. And I hope it will give you insights into what can cause a child to behave the way they do.

PERIOD PAINS: A SHAKESPEARIAN DRAMA

For many of us, puberty is a time of great misery, in part because the emotional and physical changes involved trigger past-life memories. But when you understand that the seemingly overblown responses you'll see in a teenager are spiritual as well as hormonal, it can help you deal with what's happening with greater patience and compassion.

When Adele asked me about her daughter Laura's crippling period pains, I was not surprised to find it was a past-life issue. With a strong Performer influence in her personality, I knew Laura wouldn't be one to suffer in silence.

"Does she let the world know how she's feeling?" I asked.

"So," Adele began, "Laura started menstruating when she was twelve, and she would complain in an over the top way about cramps and discomfort. I thought it was just her inner curmudgeon making a big deal of things. She would also complain about being a girl and how she'd rather be a boy because they don't have to deal with menstruation.

"What made me sit up and take notice was when we were visiting a family friend's house when Laura was 13. Laura's a martial artist and has the mentality of a 'good soldier.' But while we were there, it was the first day of her period and she couldn't keep it together.

"She was clutching her stomach and keeling over on the sofa. Her voice was faint, and she was overcome with self-pity, but my intuition said there was nothing physically wrong with her.

"We took her to a bedroom where she could lie in the dark while the rest of us ate and visited. I remember thinking, 'She's acting like she's on her deathbed.'"

To some extent, Adele was right. The pain and bleeding acted as a trigger—a reminder of her traumatic death in 1800's Scotland. Instead of calmly dealing with the onset of her period, her soul was thrown into crisis mode, fearing (irrationally) that death was imminent.

"She lay in a catatonic state for hours at our friend's house," Adele continued. "That misery during her period continued for months, and it was often hard for her to go to school on the first few days of her period. Catatonia interspersed with rants were her go-to coping methods."

To heal Laura's problem, we went back to a previous incarnation in my hometown of Aberdeen, Scotland.

At the end of that life, she'd died from loss of blood after hemorrhaging during childbirth. As her soul left her physical body behind, her sense of disappointment was acute. She felt that the doctors (particularly one who happened to be English) could have done more to save her life.

I asked Adele to tell Laura about the events surrounding her death. And I pointed out that, even if she didn't seem particularly interested, the important thing was to get through to her soul.

By the time Adele and I next spoke, things had changed dramatically.

"Laura's improvement came instantly," she said. "I had a long talk with her about the life in Aberdeen and the causes of that death. I told her everything, including how you said she blamed the doctors and felt that they could have prevented her death if they'd done better. She took it all in.

"Her next period was so different. She wasn't suffering as she usually did, and you can be sure I was watching her very closely.

"It's been over a year, and she now handles her period as a matter of course. She still has cramps, but home remedies work well for her. I had come to dread her period every month for the disruption and the Shakespearean rants on the unfairness of life and the misery of womanhood. And I'm so grateful that she no longer complains all the time about being a girl."

On the subject of her period pains, Laura described how she used to feel before the healing took place. "I was tense," she said. "Roaring with pain—groggy—like losing a waterfall of blood. My back hurt. My tummy was rock hard. I was cold, always so cold—and so tired I could sleep all day."

I asked Adele if Laura showed any other resonances from that life in Scotland. "Oh, yes," she said, "Over the years, she's made quite a few comments that seem to show her inner Scot. She went to England with a performance troupe when she was ten and, reminiscing about it, she said, "I don't know why, but every time I hear someone speak in an English accent, I just want to punch them in the face to make them shut up!'"

Healing Laura's period pains was easy. Healing her Anglophobia may take a little longer.

WHY IS THERE A HOLE IN MY STOMACH?

The following story includes a lot of detail. I want to show the many ways past-life trauma can create havoc in a family and how frustrating it can be to deal with a medical system that doesn't look beyond this life to find the cause of ailments.

Sarah's 15-year old son, James, was born with severe mental and physical issues. When we first spoke, I told her about a past life they had together. They were both young men, childhood friends, who joined the British Army to fight in the trenches of World War 1. Before setting off, they made a pact. They knew they'd probably die, but promised to always look out for one another.

One night, during the Battle of Verdun, the soul that is now Sarah was shot in the abdomen in No-Man's Land, the area between the British and German trenches. The soul who is now her son James carried his friend to safety. Sadly, he was also shot in the abdomen and died soon after. "I knew he'd saved my life!" Sarah told me.

I expected one particular problem to show up in this life. "Does James have unexplained abdominal pains?" I asked.

"He suffers excruciating pain in his stomach," she said. "He's often asked me, 'Why is there a hole in my stomach?!'"

Several years later, I received a letter from Sarah detailing her story and the profound spiritual healing that has taken place since we uncovered that past life.

"I would describe James as a pretty happy baby/child," she wrote, "But several times a week, for as long as I can remember, he would have these episodes of screaming and crying while hitting or pulling at his stomach.

"When he was a baby, his doctor switched formulas several times, prescribed drops to give him for gas, etc., but nothing seemed to make much of a difference for too long. James was always a medically fragile child, hospitalized frequently with high fevers and seizures, and was diagnosed with epilepsy at two-years old and autism at three.

"He also has severe physical and cognitive delays and was non-verbal until age four, so he couldn't articulate to me what was hurting him back then. As he got older he would take my hand and rub his stomach and say 'belly' when I would ask him why he was crying, or what hurt him."

Sarah took James to numerous doctors, neurologists, psychologists, orthopedists, and a pediatric neuropsychologist who thought James's episodes were to get attention.

She described how James would be playing happily and suddenly would start screaming and crying, hitting his stomach, becoming more and more hysterical.

"I would give him Mylanta or Tums or some other over-the-counter medication for an upset stomach, and within 10 minutes or so he would calm down, stop crying, and go back to being his happy self. And yet, as far as the doctors were concerned, nothing was physically wrong."

Sarah tried eliminating foods from his diet, took him for allergy testing, X-rays, saw a G.I. doctor, a chiropractor for adjustments, a homeopathic practitioner, a doctor who practiced alternative medicine, and even an energy healer.

"On a scale of 1 to 10, James' pain was a 9 to a 10. We kept a food diary for him to try and figure out what was happening. The neurologist thought maybe his seizure meds were upsetting his stomach. But this wasn't just a tummy ache, these were full blown crying, kicking, screaming hysterics.

"The neurologist then suggested a psychiatrist, who said

James was having anxiety attacks and prescribed Prozac. He was only about 7- or 8-years old! We tried that for a few weeks and it made no difference."

Eventually, Sarah gave up hope of ever getting help for James. She would watch what he ate, keep his clothes loose fitting around his waist, and did her best to calm him when the attacks happened.

But after speaking with me, she followed the spirit guides' advice and told James 'a story' about two best friends who went to war together. She went through the same story every night at bedtime for several weeks.

"He would just listen to me," she said. "He had no reaction to it or anything. But I guess it was within two weeks that I started noticing fewer crying episodes.

After a month, they were gone completely! This whole thing is still unbelievable to me, and I am forever grateful. It's literally been years now since James has had an episode."

I've helped many of my clients heal issues with their children by having them tell a bedtime story. Other times parents can be totally straightforward about the past-life situation, even if the preface their words with, "This may sound weird, but a psychic friend of mine told me..."

If you're a parent, it can be massively helpful to remember that your children, like you, came into this existence like fully loaded computers. Their souls carry lifetimes of experience, both good and bad, and often have huge healing they want to achieve.

IN A ROOM OF A HUNDRED PEOPLE ...

After telling Karen about how her daughter, Lola, had once been stabbed to death in a homeless shelter in New York, I asked if she showed any resonances.

Karen said, "Yes, every week, her father drives her to a homeless shelter where she's a volunteer."

This, of course, is karmic. But what blew me away is that, at the time, she was only nine years old.

Put 100 nine-year-old children in a room and how many of them, other than Lola, would, of their own accord, volunteer in a homeless shelter?

THESE ARE NOT MY PEOPLE

One of my clients told me that she never felt she belonged to her family. As a child she'd search through her parents' drawers looking for birth certificates or some other proof she was adopted.

When a child enters the world, the veil between this incarnation and others can be somewhat permeable. Children sometimes need time to get used to being in a new family and can even, like one client's four-year old daughter, pack their bags and go looking for their real mom. Usually the conscious memory of earlier lives dissipates over time but, for some, the door to the past remains open.

Remember Jane, my client from Chapter 5 whose vertigo healed after we worked together? When she and I spoke about her daughter, Ellen, it was clear that her earlier lives were as real as this life.

For Ellen, the usual separation between this plane and the next is barely there, causing her to feel a deeper connection to her past lives than to this. To get a sense of what this might be like, imagine waking up tomorrow morning in a totally different part of the world, where everyone speaks a language that's unfamiliar to you, and they expect you to fit right in.

From the time she was born, Ellen—who is now a teenager—

has believed herself to be of a different race. Though the family is of Russian extraction and lives in the Pacific Northwest, Ellen has always identified as Hispanic.

Most of her recent past lives were spent in places like Colombia, Peru, Hawaii, and in Native American communities. From what I uncovered, she'd been very badly treated by white people —from enslavement by Spanish conquistadors to being murdered by early North American settlers.

If you've been a slave in a past life, you won't respond kindly to being told what to do. As I've previously pointed out, "Don't tell me what to do!" is the motto of those who carry the memory of slavery or imprisonment. Ellen was typical of a teen with this past-life fear of Powerlessness. She'd taken her mom's car and wrecked it, and she had run away from home more than once.

All her life, Ellen has rejected her Caucasian family. From the time she was little, she would darken her skin with makeup and dye her hair black.

"People often ask me if she's adopted," Jane said. "She was always obsessed with Native American music and culture. At the age of seven, she taught herself Spanish and Hawaiian. When we visited Hawaii, she felt rejuvenated. She loved to rub dirt on her face and walk barefoot. She gets angry at being called white. She has a lot of shame about being Caucasian."

From a karmic perspective, a path that would channel the energy from her past lives would be one in which she'd become an advocate for the powerless, particularly disadvantaged Hispanic women and children. (This is a Spiritual Act—and a way to heal herself while, at the same time, helping those who suffer as she once did.)

When I interviewed her mother for this book, I asked, "How is Ellen doing?"

"She's wonderful!" Jane said. "She's finishing up her medical interpreting course, and though she was the only non-Hispanic student, she quickly earned the respect of the staff and students.

She wants to help Spanish speakers, especially women and children. She's dating a Hispanic boy who she adores. His family loves her. They call her 'the girl with the Mexican soul.'"

For anyone who identifies strongly with a certain group of people, it's important to follow the soul's desire to help them in some way. It's a way to balance the karma from previous lives.

HEALING NIGHT TERRORS

Many children have nightmares that go back to past-life trauma. A sign that they're related to a specific experience is that they tend to be recurring. Once you find the original past-life trauma, you can create healing, even in an infant, by telling them what happened. Even if the conscious mind doesn't get it, the soul will.

Nine-year old Donovan had a past life as a British soldier stationed in Hamburg shortly after WWII. He was traveling in a truck when it hit a landmine on the road. He was thrown clear, but his legs were badly damaged. His friends were trapped in the wreckage, and he could only watch helplessly as they died. He was shipped out to a hospital in southern England where surgeons amputated his right leg.

Donovan's mother, Helen, said, "That explains why he's always had pain in his right leg. I have to rub it at night before he goes to sleep."

It was sleep, however, that was Donovan's biggest challenge. "He's always had night terrors," his mother said. "It doesn't just affect him, but has been extremely disruptive for the whole family. In his nightmares, he screams and cries, calling out for help for people who are trapped." [A clear reference to the event in Germany.]

Helen told me later, "That night, after speaking with you, he had the night terrors again. He spoke of the people that are trapped and how he couldn't get them out. I reassured him that they're no longer trapped. I said, 'They're free and safe, and so are you.' I let him know that it's over, it's not happening now, and how that was then, and this is now. The next night was totally peaceful. He got a full night's sleep, and he's never had a single night terror since then."

AN EDWARDIAN GIRL IN A 21ST CENTURY BODY

The light from distant stars can take billions of years to reach us, which means we see them as they were a long time ago. In a child, the light from their past lives often shines brightly, allowing us to see them as they were sometimes hundreds of years in the past. As I've said before, past lives explain everything. But in the case of this 14-year-old, one particular past life outshines every other.

Holly asked me about the death of her husband and how it had affected their daughter, Eloise. There was an obvious fear of loss from a previous life that manifested as an exaggerated fear of losing her mother, but the spirit guides felt there was so much more to uncover.

"Eloise is an Edwardian girl in a 21st Century body," they told me. She was born into a wealthy English family in the late 1800s. The family had servants, but because her soul had also been a servant in an earlier life, she identified with them. Unlike others in her family, she was always respectful towards them.

As a girl growing up as part of the English aristocracy, she was expected to be ladylike, but she had a lot of masculine energy in her. Having a rough-and-tumble upbringing with her two older brothers made her something of a tomboy. She was empowered by a belief handed down from her grandmother in that life who always said, "You can do anything in this life."

Holly confirmed a number of points. Eloise is extremely polite and will berate her mother if she feels she's insufficiently respectful to a store clerk. She's also something of a tomboy in this life, too.

Since Eloise had once been a servant, there was one resonance I expected. "Does she work really hard?" I asked.

"Oh, yes," Holly replied. "She feels she has to work hard all the time."

The spirit guides continued by describing a significant event from that past life. When the girl was 16, an older boy reached under her dress and touched her inappropriately. She responded by swinging a small table at him and knocking him flat.

Holly laughed. "I always wondered where her anger came from. She's so well-mannered and sweet, but she's not afraid to stand up for herself."

"Is she uncomfortable being touched?" I asked.

"She's never liked being touched," Holly said. "As a baby, you couldn't kiss her. I used to say you could kiss the air around her, but you couldn't kiss her face."

It's worth mentioning that souls want to be touched. So, if your baby or child hates to be hugged, don't worry, it's probably not you, it's a past-life problem.

The spirit guides were not finished with Eloise's past life. They described how the girl grew up flouting convention by wearing men's suits in the hope of putting men off. After her brothers died in World War I, she moved to a small market town where, despite a huge trust fund, she lived frugally in almost complete isolation, afraid her money wouldn't last as long as she would.

"Does she internalize her emotions or isolate herself?" I asked.

"Oh yes. After her father died, she wouldn't talk about him or his death and absolutely refused go to therapy."

"Is she afraid of not having enough money?" I wondered.

"She hoards money! She has wads of hundreds. She won't spend any of it, and she won't let me spend money when we're out. She's on top of every penny."

And then we examined the end of that past life. In the 1950s, she fulfilled a lifelong dream by taking a trip to India. Sadly, she caught typhoid fever from contaminated food and died on the sea voyage home.

When a soul associates travel with not returning from whence it started, it will usually prefer to stay put.

"Does Eloise hate to travel?" I asked.

"Absolutely!" her mother said, "She's a total homebody."

And when a soul relates food to death, it becomes hypersensitive to what it allows the body to ingest.

"Is she particular about food? Does it have to be fresh?"

"Food, oh my God!" Holly exclaimed. "One little piece of mold on her toast the other day and she flipped out. She never eats leftovers."

As we came to the end of the exploration, I said to Holly, "Eloise seems to be profoundly connected to that past life."

She said, "Yes, and do you know what's funny? When she was younger, people actually said she looked like an Edwardian girl!"

YOU'RE FREAKING ME OUT!

When I worked with 23-year-old Erin, I found a disturbing event from a past life. As a man in World War II, she'd been tied to a chair and interrogated.

I told her, "Your chest was cut repeatedly with a knife. Are you sensitive about that area of your body?"

Erin shrieked, "Oh my God, you're freaking me out! I can't bear to have anyone touch my chest. I can't even examine my own breasts without throwing up, and I will *never* have a mammogram!"

Erin's mother, Danielle, is also a client of mine. The next time I spoke to her, she said "Erin told me about the past life. It's amazing. From the moment she was born, she would never let me touch her chest. I always wondered why."

A few years later, Danielle reported that Erin has lost her fear of breast examinations. Although they are, as she put it, "Not her favorite thing to do," she no longer goes into a panic at the mere idea of having one.

TRAUMA ON DISPLAY

When a child acts out, behaves obnoxiously, or pushes all your buttons, it's easy to throw up your hands and walk away from them. However, the behavior you dislike in your child is almost always a manifestation of the past-life trauma they carry with them, and that's why it's important to exercise compassion.

Pamela's daughter entered this life with a massive fear of Rejection, stemming from death on a Central American battlefield in an earlier life.

I described to her the symptoms I'd expect in a 14-year old dealing with this awful memory.

"Her soul believes itself to be unlovable." I began. "Dying in violent circumstances, a long way from home, her soul left the planet carrying the conscious mind's belief that it had been abandoned by God and humanity. It may not be logical. These things rarely are. But right now, her soul is trying to prove it's not worthy of love. Does she push you away?"

"All the time," Pamela said.

"If you allow her to do that, you give her what she wants. If you appear to reject her, she wins. Her soul can say, "A-ha! I knew you didn't really love me!"

No soul comes into the world without fear, and it doesn't take much to trigger traumatic memories from hundreds of years back. But there's always a solution, and one of the simplest is for your actions to match your words.

It sounds almost too simple, but let me give you an analogy:

If your father said, "I'll always be there for you," but forgot to turn up for your graduation, and never remembered your birthday, what message do you think he'd have given you? It's probably not one of congruity.

But if he'd said, "I'll always be there for you," and always was, you'll have believed him. And most important, you'll have interpreted his consistency as love.

Children need love. And they need to know that it's unconditional—that no matter what happens, you'll always love them. If your love is dependent on their behavior, the past-life fears will soon convince the child's soul that it's not worthy of love.

I have a client whose son committed armed robbery, more than one whose child "borrowed" and wrecked the family car, and one whose teenage daughter punched a cop. Sadly, I have many clients whose children are dealing with serious drug addiction and all that that entails.

These kids' parents have stayed in a loving place because they recognize that loving someone doesn't mean condoning their behavior. To express disapproval by rejecting their children would be to act contrary to their soul's core values.

Whether you're struggling with your child's issues, or your own trauma from childhood, the deepest healing begins when you explore the past lives that cause emotional molehills in this life to erupt into volcanoes.

EXERCISE: WHAT HAPPENED TO YOU?

List three fears, blocks, phobias, quirks, or other challenges you see in your child or children, or that you remember from your own childhood.

Now, think about the question, "What happened to you or them?" Then make a list of what might have happened in a past life to cause these beliefs or behaviors. Don't sweat it! Simply allow the words to come out.

Spend as much time processing this as feels right, and when you're done, remind your soul "that was then, this is now." If it's your child's past life, consider sharing it with them either verbatim, or as an age appropriate story.

Children, just like adults, have an enormous amount of baggage they carry with them. Unfortunately, their past–life trauma can show up in ways that disempower them. I'm sure we've all, at some point, heard a child say, "I just can't do it!" or, "I'll never be any good at..." They're simply expressing their soul's past-life fear of Failure.

Yet, to the best of its ability, no soul will tolerate (regardless of how old you are) allowing its past-life experiences to interfere with achieving everything it has planned for this lifetime.

11

LIVING AN EMPOWERED LIFE

AVOIDING THE TRAP OF VICTIMIZATION

*I*t's been thousands of years since your soul left the Causal Plane for the rough and tumble of life on Earth. And in that time, you've had many incarnations where you were put down, disempowered, and treated as if you didn't matter. When those experiences were significant enough to take you off your life plan, they left a wound you may still carry with you now.

If you ever go into a place of defeat, you've got this wound. If you feel disempowered, overwhelmed by life's challenges, or helpless to change your circumstances, it's a sign you're slipping into a place of victimization rather than empowerment.

LEAH'S STORY

Leah contacted me days after leaving her partner due to domestic violence. By the time we spoke, she'd already gone to the police, but was second-guessing herself about whether to get a restraining order. She feared an angry backlash, or that he'd follow through with his threats of suicide.

She asked, "Is there some action I should take to honor our soul contract? What can I do or trust in this situation?"

The spirit guides were adamant from their opening remarks. "Trust is irrevocably broken," they said. "He has violated every aspect of your Mutual Support agreement."

A Mutual Support agreement is one of the most common between two souls. It's meant to ensure that the relationship feels balanced and that both are pulling equal weight. In Leah's case, the agreement was now, as the spirit guides put it, "null and void."

"Abuse," they explained, "Is something humans don't always recognize. We encourage you to use that term without shame or embarrassment." They also pointed out that when a person's safety is threatened, they can't support a relationship. Their purpose—as well as guidance—is to protect.

"He threatened your life. That's as serious as it gets. It's entirely his karma, not yours," I told Leah. And then I paused, realizing the guides wanted to emphasize the point. "The guides have repeated that three times to be sure you hear it, know it, and believe it. It's entirely his karma, not yours. He has responsibility for the consequences of his actions."

The guides had more observations and a suggestion for moving forward. First, Leah's heart chakra had taken a real battering, and they recommended she spend time being around people who would love, care for, and nurture her.

To help her get unstuck and begin looking forward, the guides suggested she take stock of her life. "Think about what you want your future to look like," they suggested. "Make a list of ten things. Have fun with this exercise and don't overthink it."

From a practical standpoint, the guides reminded Leah that there's a system in place to protect and support people in her situation. She was reminded that she could trust people and processes that had protocols: attorneys, therapists, the police.

Due to a past-life fear of Inferiority, Leah struggled with self-worth. I described to her how the fear causes its many sufferers to settle in a relationship. They'll say things like, "It's not that bad, at least he doesn't hit me."

The positive lesson she could draw from this experience was about taking care of herself. The spirit guides gave her an empowering phrase to use as a kind of affirmation: "I won't allow myself to be pushed around. I will stand up for myself."

"Thank you so much for the messages," Leah told me. "I feel relieved and stronger, like my soul let go and can move on. 'The agreement is null and void, entirely his karma not mine.' Saying it three times made such a difference. I can now recognize the abuse after being in denial for so long. I can have compassion for his pain but know I can never trust him again."

Practical spirituality happens when you help a fellow soul who is going through a rough patch, or who needs help getting their power back after a crisis. Leah needed a safe space where her ex couldn't find her, so my wife and I offered her the use of our guest room for as long as she needed it.

One of Leah's lessons is to learn to accept help when it's offered. And one of ours will always be to model what it means to be compassionate old souls.

The day she moved in, I brought my teenage children up to speed with what had happened. "I don't think you're in any danger," I said, "But I totally understand if you'd prefer to stay at your mom's for a while." To their credit, both my kids said they were not going to be intimidated by any abuser. They were staying put.

KARMIC PATTERNS

We all have past lives of victimization and disempowerment behind us. The triggers and reminders from those lives show up when we're most challenged and can rob us of our ability to recognize how strong we really are. Unfortunately, when you're in that place of powerlessness, the light at the end of the tunnel may be almost impossible to see.

One of my past lives was as an opium addict in China in the 1800s, and resonances from that incarnation have shown up a lot this time around. Because my addiction led to tragic consequences for my family back then, in this life, I fell into a pattern of feeling responsible for everyone else's happiness and wellbeing.

When you see patterns showing up in your life, pay attention. It's very likely a sign you're caught in a kind of karmic loop. If you can say, "I *always* seem to..." As in "I *always* seem to find emotionally unavailable partners," or "I *always* seem to end up with difficult bosses," it's the sign of a karmic pattern.

My soul chose to draw in important lessons around addiction to help me balance the consequences of my behavior in China. By choosing an alcoholic father and being affected by someone else's addiction, my soul hoped to see the other side of the karmic coin. But the experience is not the lesson, and I failed to draw the necessary lessons from being around my dad.

What should the lessons have been? Ideally, I should have learned to take care of myself instead of taking responsibility for everyone else. But I grew up covering for my dad, lying to my mother when he asked me to, and fighting her battles with him as if they were my own. I'd never heard the word codependent, but I could have written a book about it.

In a perfect world, I should have learned to avoid repeating the experience of being victimized by someone else's addiction. But I didn't. And nor do many adult children of alcoholic parents. I spent a big chunk of my life with alcoholic partners. It was, to some extent, all I knew.

Not everyone who constantly ends up in alcoholic relationships is balancing karma from past lives, of course. But they often are. Patterns tell you what you're working on. I spent years trying to keep my parents' marriage together and stayed in dysfunctional relationships well past their expiration dates in the belief that somehow, through the power of love and good intentions, I could fix decades of someone's addiction or mental illness.

And how did this idealistic approach work? Not so well. Then, at a particularly stressful point, the spirit guides pointed out, "There's a big difference between supporting someone and enabling them."

What I was working on was not just seeing the consequences of someone else's addiction. It was to heal the past-life fear of Inferiority that kept me in a place of disempowerment. (Sometimes things seem too hard to change, so it becomes easier to find coping strategies rather than getting to the root of a problem.)

In a past life, I'd been a boy in Lucknow, India, who'd had a miserable life as a result of disempowerment through dyslexia, illiteracy, and poverty. My life ended in a state of complete powerlessness.

If you have a past life like this, and it's not usually too hard to find something similar, you can easily slip into the habit of blaming others or failing to see the common denominator in your patterns: you!

When you notice patterns, the important thing is to change your behavior. If you can step back and recognize the patterns you're repeating, you're on the way to breaking the karmic spell.

So, if you keep running into infidelity, dishonesty, drama, verbal abuse, violence, gaslighting, neglect, addiction, anger, control, or whatever, then remember to look in the mirror.

What aspect of your behavior is drawing in the repetitive experiences? And what might you change in yourself to break the patterns?

Recognizing the past-life source of my patterns began a process of healing. I gradually removed my people-pleasing mask to reveal a feistier, more self-empowered persona reflective of the true person I am. And it's a process you or anyone else can do.

When you look at the part you play in your relationships (and remember, it takes two) think about what might have happened in a past life to make you the way you are. If you're afraid to speak up, for example, might you have been persecuted at one time for your beliefs? Then think about what you can do to change. Visualize common situations you find yourself in, and see yourself speaking with confidence and authority.

YOU ALWAYS HAVE OPTIONS

Sometimes I'll work with someone who has become so disempowered they can't see the most appalling circumstances for what they are. One client complained, "My husband uses me for sex any time he wants. I'll be cooking dinner, and he'll just bend me over the table and force himself on me."

When I asked, "Why do you let him?" she said, "Because he gets really angry if I don't. I can't stop him." When I told her this was rape, not only did she initially disagree, but was angry with me for even suggesting it. And when I told her she had options, like going to the authorities, she said that was out of the question because it would upset the children and, anyway, it would only enrage him if she did.

It's easy to see abuse in someone else's life. Unfortunately, it can be a lot harder to recognize it in your own. Many people get into an abusive situation at work or in a relationship and fail to notice how bad things are until they reach a crisis point.

It's not unusual to carry powerlessness from our past life experiences. Having been imprisoned or enslaved, even hundreds of years ago, you can still be unable to see the full range of options available to you now.

Throw into the mix a past-life fear of Inferiority, the result of a life in which you were victimized by someone or something, and you can easily slip into a place of victimization now.

This was exactly what happened to Lori, who I first spoke to in 2008 at the height of the financial crisis. As she put it, "I feel permanently stuck." Her marriage was supremely unsatisfying, and her job sucked.

I asked her, "What have you done to change things?"

Lori replied, "Nothing. There's nothing I can do. If I try to talk to my husband, he just yells at me. And I'm never going to get another job the way things are right now."

My spirit guides are well aware that we on the Physical Plane have to deal with everyday challenges, and they always want to help us find solutions. Yet, as they often point out, they can't wave a magic wand and restore an entire economy to how it once was. They can, however, see options when we're unable to so much as glimpse the light at the end of the proverbial tunnel.

Unfortunately for Lori, she couldn't make any forward movement because there seemed to be no decision without the potential for disaster.

"If I quit my job," she said, "I could lose everything. And if I leave my husband, I'll lose my home."

The spirit guides, however, wanted her to see that there might be other ways. "What do you want in your life?" they asked.

She was silent. After a long pause, she said, "I don't know."

And so began a conversation about empowerment. From the spirit guides' perspective, Lori was disempowered because she was stuck in a place of victimization. If she could escape the invisible chains of powerlessness, she'd find there was a lot she could do to change her circumstances.

"Are you happy in your work?" the spirit guides asked.

Lori was unambiguous. "I hate it."

"Are you fulfilled in your marriage?"

"No," she said, "It's not working for me."

"What's wrong with the relationship?" I asked.

"He's totally disrespectful," Lori said. "If I complain about things, he yells. If I try to talk about how I feel, he makes fun of me. And if I suggest we get a divorce, he tells me that will never happen."

The spirit guides had a solution, which began as a question. "What are your needs?" Lori was at the other end of the phone, but I could picture her face as she said, "I really don't know."

NEEDS? WHAT NEEDS?

I can tell someone has a past-life fear of Inferiority because if I ask them, "What are your needs?" they stare blankly, like a deer in the headlights. Most often, they've never had the luxury of putting themselves first, so they have no idea what things are important to them and, therefore, little chance of manifesting them.

"The first step is to identify your needs," the spirit guides said. "What are three needs you have in your marriage?"

With a little coaching, Lori saw that three of her most fundamental needs related to the problems she'd identified earlier. "I want to be respected," she began.

The spirit guides corrected her. "You need…" they said.

"I need to be respected. I need to be spoken to kindly. I need to be heard."

Those three statements became Lori's mantra and also formed the basis of a conversation she had a few days later with her husband.

And when we talked again, almost a year later, her life had changed.

"It wasn't easy," she said, "But I kept confronting him, over and over again, telling him I needed him to listen to me and respect me. And after one scary outburst, I told him that if he ever raised his voice to control me again, that I'd walk out and go straight to a divorce lawyer!"

Although I had no recollection of this part of the conversation when we first spoke, Lori told me the spirit guides had asked her what she was doing to find another job, and when she replied, "Nothing," they'd said, "Then do something!" Almost immediately, she'd begun sending out her resume. Three months later, she had a new job.

Whether or not Lori would stay in either her marriage or her new position was not certain, but whatever happened, the choices she would make would come from a place of empowerment, not victimization.

Lori turned her life around, and the changes began by identifying her needs, and recognizing that she had more options than she thought. Stepping outside of the victim role takes effort, and the rewards are always worth it. But it's not just people who have the power to put you in a place of victimization.

WHEN SUBSTANCES VICTIMIZE YOU

Andrea was enslaved in a past life. Typically, she doesn't take too kindly to being told what to do. The problem is that one-time slaves can carry past-life fears of Inferiority and Powerlessness, a combination that can easily put them into a place of victimization.

When they become victimized by such things as food, alcohol, drugs or, in Andrea's case, cigarettes, they can feel helpless to overcome their addiction.

By the time I spoke to Andrea, she'd tried everything to quit smoking: nicotine patches, gum, hypnotism, and even cold laser therapy—twice. She said. "The reality is that I'm never going to quit," The one thing she hadn't tried, however, was past-life exploration. It turned out that her decades-long addiction to tobacco was related to a past life as a slave worker in a factory in Poland during World War II.

As we wound up her session, my spirit guides suggested she'd have better luck giving up smoking if she kept a pack in plain sight. It would prevent her soul from feeling it was being deprived.

When I next spoke to Andrea, she was excited to tell me what had happened. "Soon after my session—maybe within two weeks —and without even trying, it's like the habit just fell away.

"I can't put into words how big of a miracle this is. I haven't smoked since November of 2016. On almost a daily basis, I'm in awe that I no longer have this habit that dictates when I have to go outside for a smoke break or away from others just to feed a nicotine craving. It's a freedom I never thought I could experience again."

After a past life of slavery, many people have a heightened need for personal freedom. Ironically, they begin smoking as an expression of freedom, but end up becoming victims once again. Healing her soul's past-life trauma allowed Andrea to unshackle herself from the chains of her addiction and experience true freedom.

EXERCISE: THREE STEPS TO SELF-EMPOWERMENT

Your soul and your spirit guides will never support your staying in a place of victimization; in fact, their job is to get you out of it as quickly as possible.

Have you ever woken up after bingeing on something you knew was not good for you—like a gallon of ice cream or a bottle of Jack Daniels—and felt that you just couldn't wait to do it again? If your overindulgence triggered soul-level memories of victimization, then probably not. It's more likely that you felt remorse or even shame.

Your soul will imbue your conscious self with good feelings when you act in a positive, self-empowered way and negative feelings when you don't.

You'll never hear anyone say, "I used to feel so much better about myself when I was letting people mistreat me." Self-empowerment feels good. And remember, you always have the power of the universe behind you when you choose to be empowered.

As you've seen, recognizing your options is a powerful way to become empowered. For this exercise, I want you to do the following:

- **Step 1:** Take any one problem or difficult situation you're dealing with. Describe the problem in one sentence.
- **Step 2:** Write ten things you can do to alleviate, remedy, alter, change, or transform the situation.
- **Step 3:** Start doing them!

You're never a victim of your past lives, just as you're never totally a victim of sugar, tobacco, alcohol, an abusive boss, or a domineering spouse. And when you walk through the world in a state of self-empowerment rather than one of victimization, you'll find yourself tapping into one of your soul's highest values: that of respect.

PEACE, LOVE, AND UNDERSTANDING

WALKING THE TALK OF OLD-SOUL VALUES

*I*n the song of the same name, Elvis Costello asked, "What's so funny 'bout peace, love, and understanding?" I'll tell you the answer: Nothing! Peace, love, and understanding are three of your soul's highest values.

But, in a world run by younger souls, lip service is all that may be paid to these ideals. Those who have yet to learn the important lessons that will eventually lead them to embrace peace, love, and understanding are often the ones who talk the talk but nothing more.

Sanctimonious young-soul politicians (and an unfortunate number of old souls, too) will say they regret the loss of civilian life—as they continue to blow up people in other countries to supposedly bring peace. Yet, if peace was really the objective, then war would never be the answer.

You don't want bombs dropping on your head. As an old soul, you'll want every opportunity to complete your life plan without violent interruption, and you'll be far more likely to realize that others deserve the same. Young souls want to avoid getting blown up just as much as you do, but they've still to learn to extend that courtesy to others.

If younger souls valued peace, they wouldn't attack other countries, murder innocents to further their narrow political or religious agendas, or counter violence with more violence. And if they valued love, they'd see violence as its antithesis. How can you espouse love while terrorizing or blowing up others? You can't. Not, at least, without a huge amount of hypocrisy or cognitive dissonance.

Understanding is gained through empathy. And that's something souls develop over many, many lifetimes. When you understand someone, you can empathize with them, and that means you no longer see them as any different from yourself.

What's so funny about peace, love, and understanding? Again, nothing. These fundamental, core values have been learned over the span of many incarnations. They are the markers of older, wiser souls, and are values to which every one of us should aspire.

WHY EVERYTHING IS POLITICAL

After publishing an article a few years ago, I received an e-mail that read: *"I really wish you would stay out of American politics, Ainslie!!!"*

I have absolutely no plans to stay out of politics. And neither should you. Spirituality and politics are inseparable, and it's the responsibility of all old souls to be involved, and not allow younger, less experienced souls to run the world and its institutions.

Your soul, like every other soul, wants to reach the end of this life and look back on it with a sense of accomplishment—knowing you left the world a little better for having been here. And that means being involved in worldly affairs.

You don't *have* to get involved. You have free will, after all. You can climb a mountain and spend your life in meditation, blissfully separating yourself from the rest of humanity. It's your choice. But is that really spiritual?

If you ask most people to think of three great spiritual leaders, they'll give you names like Martin Luther King, Mahatma Gandhi, and Jesus. What do these three individuals have in common? I'll give you a clue—it's not political apathy.

Martin Luther King, Mahatma Gandhi, and Jesus were all deeply spiritual beings. And they were major forces for social change. How different would our world be if these old souls had shrugged their shoulders in the face of injustice and said, "I'm not really interested in politics"?

Unfortunately, a lot of older souls struggle with political apathy. Faced with a system that causes them to feel powerless, almost half the U.S. population doesn't even bother to vote. And who can blame them? As a friend of mine says, "No matter who you vote for, the government always gets in."

STALIN WAS RIGHT

Soviet dictator Joseph Stalin is reputed to have said, "The people who cast the votes decide nothing; the people who count the votes decide everything."

In the U.S., as with most countries, the voting system is flawed and corrupt. Security experts found the machines that count the vote can literally "be opened with the key from a hotel minibar and hacked within minutes." And few measures have been taken to prevent hackers from foreign countries tampering with numbers.

In an old-soul world, these kinds of things would not be tolerated.

Just because they feel politically impotent, doesn't mean old souls should just give up on the whole thing. Whether we choose to be a part of the political process or not is entirely up to us. We all have free will. It's a question of choice. But it's important to be aware, when making our choice, that we're all passengers on the same train, whether we like it or not.

Practical spirituality is all about improving the lot of others. Can you be a truly spiritual person without applying your spirituality in some way?

You don't (as I've stated several times) have to be Mother Teresa to make a difference. But there is a spiritual imperative to help create a better world. It may be something monumental like saving orphans in Uganda, or it may be as simple as contributing a few dollars to charity.

As an old soul, it's incumbent upon you to act from a place of love as much and as often as you possibly can. Ignoring what's happening in the outside world—while an understandable coping mechanism—is political apathy, with fear at the root.

Being informed, and helping to make this world a better place, is acting from a place of love. It is, of course, your choice.

And if you wonder where to channel your energy, think about what upsets you or fires you up. We are all triggered in some way by the experience of others.

When you get moved by the sight of homeless children, for example, your soul will scan its past lives for a frame of reference. If you were once a homeless and hungry child, your soul will use your own experience to inspire action.

Whether you're moved to help stray dogs, blind people, victims of famine, refugees, child prostitutes, or political prisoners, the important thing is to recognize that over the course of centuries, you've been there. And what would you have wanted back then? Someone to help you. Now you can be that person.

PEACE

I became a pacifist in my teen years. I joined the Peace Pledge Union, and signed the pledge stating that I'd never support or sanction war. Since then, I've frequently been called to defend my position. I'm asked, "Nobody wants war, but isn't it sometimes necessary?"

My argument is that if I said, "I'm totally against domestic violence," I'm sure you'd agree with me. But if I said, "I'm totally against domestic violence but, you know, sometimes they leave you no choice," then I imagine you'd be appalled.

To me there are no mitigating circumstances. I'm opposed to violence whether it comes from a soldier or a domestic abuser. Taking a peaceful approach to conflict does not mean allowing yourself to be bullied, trampled upon, or used. As I pointed out in the previous chapter, your soul always wants you to be empowered, not victimized. You have every right to protect yourself and defend those who are unable to defend themselves.

THE WARRIOR

Armies are full of action-oriented Hunter types. They are the ones best suited for such a rugged life. But the purpose of Hunters is to protect, defend, and ensure the survival, of the tribe. Spiritually, they are supported in using force only in defense. The belligerent Warrior is a corruption of the Hunter.

Your soul will always guide you to seek a peaceful solution to every conflict, whether it's global, or just between you and one other person.

Aggression as a means to deal with conflict is fear-based, and often the easy way. It takes strength to take the peaceful approach.

The person who resorts to aggression, anger, or violence to control the outcome of a situation has, in spiritual terms, failed. Yet, we live in a world where aggression surrounds us. We see it in movies and television, of course, but we also see it in those in positions of power.

The spirit guides won't waiver in their insistence that war is never acceptable. We live in a belligerent world, but it doesn't have to be that way, and it won't always be. It's important to recognize that when someone tells you there's no option other than armed conflict, they're wrong. Every war is one of choice. You might argue that there's no choice if you're being attacked. Yet what about peaceful, nonviolent action as an alternative? Studies show that nonviolent campaigns in support of democracy are over twice as successful as violent campaigns, and take an average of two years as opposed to eight.

Deep down, the old soul might feel that armed aggression is not the right answer, but can often be convinced by others that they're somehow being naïve, lacking in courage, unpatriotic, or are ignorant of all the facts. It's not that they lack the courage of their convictions, but that their beliefs are not validated or reinforced by the majority.

If we lived in a more peaceful world—one in which nonviolence was mainstream—old souls would have their beliefs reinforced by others all the time. It would help to truly make violence the last resort.

LOVE

Love is the soul's ultimate goal. Determining your values is a lot easier when you can ask yourself the question, "Am I acting from a place of love?" Defining love is not easy, but you can think of it as compassion, kindness, and even altruism.

Your soul wants to take the loving path in every circumstance. Sadly, however, the expression of love is suppressed in many younger-soul cultures as it's confused with weakness, sentimentality, and feminine energy. Boys are trained not to cry, men are admired for hiding their emotions, and the open expression of true love is so often frowned upon.

In this young-soul world, even the oldest souls may be reticent to fully express their true emotions. Think about it. Has there ever been a time when you really wanted to tell someone how much you loved them, but you didn't because it didn't seem appropriate?

Although there are souls in this world who have all the love they need, almost every soul seeks greater love from its fellow souls. All of us need to be loved, to feel that we matter, and to be understood.

UNDERSTANDING

Understanding is achieved through empathy, a quality developed through lifetimes of experience. With empathy we can see the humanity in others and recognize that their suffering is no different from our own. Understanding is not intellectual, in that you can't study to become empathetic.

The deepest empathy is learned from lifetimes as a Caregiver type, particularly because it requires communicating on a more intuitive level with those who can't easily express themselves verbally. This includes babies and children, the sick and dying, those who are cognitively impaired, and animals.

Understanding is an expression of love. Who doesn't feel a little warmer and fuzzier when someone truly gets you? Yet, like all expressions of love, younger souls and those who are blocked in the area of the heart chakra don't always value it.

EMPATHY AND JUSTICE

Back in 2009, when President Barack Obama nominated Judge Sonia Sotomayor for a position on the U.S. Supreme Court, he stated, "I view that quality of empathy, of understanding and identifying with people's hopes and struggles, as an essential ingredient for arriving at just decisions and outcomes."

The idea of empathy being a desirable quality in a judge had Level 5 soul Rush Limbaugh complain, "Obama has said, 'We need people with empathy.' No, we don't!"

Of course, someone like Limbaugh, who ducked military service on account of anal cysts, would have no such qualms about receiving empathy when it came to saving his own backside. Such hypocrisy is actually a sign of the absence of empathy.

All souls are tribal. We're hardwired that way. Thousands of years ago, identifying with others like us helped keep the tribe together. Now, that need to belong is what both unites and divides us. The younger the soul, the easier it is to slip into a place of suspicion. Yet it doesn't have to be that way.

As a teenager, I met an inspirational old soul by the name of Ruth Dayan. If you're familiar with the history of the Middle East, you might remember her first husband, Israeli general Moshe Dayan, who wore a distinctive black eye-patch and came to international attention during the Six-Day War of 1967.

In a part of the world in which young souls are armed to the teeth, where Israelis and Palestinians have been in conflict for almost a century, Ruth befriended Raymonda Tawil, a fellow humanitarian, who would eventually become mother-in-law to Yasser Arafat, the leader of the Palestinian Liberation Organization.

Though their husbands perceived themselves to be at opposite ends of some imaginary spectrum, their wives became best friends, united in the search to find common ground between their two tribes. A BBC article about the two women described their friendship as "a testament to our human capacity to reach out to one another even in the darkest times."

When you develop a close connection with someone, you create the opportunity to merge through your heart chakras. This leads to intimacy and then to understanding. Again, understanding is not something done in the analytical part of the brain, it's achieved through the heart.

Empathy, the key to understanding, is a talent, in that it's something learned and developed over many lifetimes. That's why you don't hear an old soul like the Dalai Lama calling for airstrikes on Middle-Eastern countries in the same way you do with young-soul talking heads on FOX News.

The talent for Empathy imbues you with the ability to pick up on non-verbal emotional signals. It allows you put yourself in another person's shoes and to feel what they're feeling. It's a form of communication as valid as speech. If you're paying attention, it will give you a nose for sniffing out dishonesty better than any lie detector.

When someone congratulates you on a wonderful success—while simultaneously seething with jealousy—it's your talent for empathy that tells you something's not right. The non-verbal emotional signals don't match the spoken word. The gulf between the two is an incongruity that can be felt emotionally, often in your body.

When someone is truly happy for you, there's no incongruity. The verbal and non-verbal signals are in harmony. It's like when you're tuning into a radio station and you get a perfect signal.

As an old soul, it's your responsibility to act with congruity. That means engaging your empathy and taking a peaceful approach to ending conflict, whether it's between individuals or between nations.

FORGIVENESS

Think of the most spiritual people you know. Do they harbor bitterness towards others? Do they go home at night and stick pins in voodoo dolls to punish their coworkers? It's extremely unlikely.

Spirituality is synonymous with peace, love, and understanding. Someone who truly embodies these core values will walk the talk. And, when they don't, it's usually not long before the empathic BS detector in others tells them the radio is not tuned to the station.

Understanding leads to forgiveness, which is a practice that can benefit every one of us. It's not always easy, as I'm sure you know.

Some of the hurts we carry go so deep that the idea of forgiving the perpetrator can seem unthinkable. And if you find it impossible to forgive someone, don't blame yourself. You've not failed some spiritual test.

Forgiveness is a way to move yourself out of the past and into the present. It releases the resentments that pile up over the years. It's never about condoning bad behavior. Forgiveness is not something you can fake. It is, however, a practice you can cultivate. And forgiveness opens your heart chakra to love.

My father was an alcoholic until almost his last days, when dementia caused him to forget where he kept the corkscrew. When my mother was close to her passing, she reflected on her decision to stick with him (she wished she hadn't) despite his occasionally abusive behavior.

But she told me something that had helped her forgive him,

and it helped me better understand what had made him the way he was and forgive him too.

When he was ten years old, my father watched his older brothers get an undeserved telling off from their minister father for pilfering the communion wine.

"It's not the stealing that I mind," he told them, "It's the fact you won't admit it."

Nobody thought to smell the breath of the youngest member of the family. Knowing my father had a penchant for alcohol at an early age doesn't excuse any bad behavior he displayed in his later years, but it goes some way toward explaining it.

The more you know about someone, the more you see their humanity. And, of course, that makes forgiveness easier. Regularly practicing forgiveness helps to keep you in a compassionate place, and that's why it's such an important thing for you to do.

It can be useful to regularly review your feelings about people and events in your life. The experience is not the lesson, but what you choose to draw from it. Processing leads to understanding.

One of my major lessons in this life has been to develop compassion for those who struggle with addictive behavior and mental illness. Understanding that mission, and learning that no soul wants to hurt another played a big part in helping me to release resentment and reach a place of compassion.

Forgiveness is an expression of love. As author Anne McCaffrey wrote, "Make no judgments where you have no compassion."

When a person behaves towards you in a way that's hurtful or baffling, ask yourself, "I wonder what made them that way?" Actively use your curiosity to trigger your empathy.

Now, there are circumstances where someone has done something so egregious that forgiveness might be next to impossible. And timing can be important. As the spirit guides point out, it can be hard to forgive a mugger while you're being mugged.

Few people are all bad (or, of course, all good), and you have a choice regarding where you focus your attention. Take the spiritual high road. It's the old-soul way.

As I said, no soul wants to hurt another. When someone does you harm, it's never with their soul's blessing.

EXERCISE: FORGIVING THOSE WHO HAVE HURT YOU

By offering another person forgiveness, you take the spiritual high road while simultaneously releasing the energetic millstone of resentment from around your neck. Forgiveness, I should stress, doesn't mean condoning someone's bad behavior, or not holding them accountable.

A powerful way to heal the hurts you carry is to use the exercise I describe as my spirit guides' version of the Hawaiian practice of reconciliation and forgiveness known as *ho'oponopono*. It goes like this:

- Make a list of people who have hurt you.
- With your eyes closed, picture each one about a foot from your face.
- Say twice: "I love you and forgive you."
- Allow the image to fade, dissolve or crumble.
- Repeat with the next person on the list.

This exercise is simple, yet profound. One client, who'd experienced some of the worst treatment of anyone I've ever worked with, told me this was the most effective thing she'd done to move past the hurts. Many others have expressed surprise that it took such little effort to gain such incredible healing.

You may find you only have to do this exercise once, but it

won't hurt to do it as often as you feel necessary. It works for little hurts and big ones equally, and goes a long way towards healing and opening your heart chakra as well.

THE BEST LIFE EVER

I made the final edits to this book while recovering from open-heart surgery to repair a faulty valve. When people would ask me if I was worried about having surgery, I'd tell them, "I'm more concerned about what will happen if I don't." (According to my cardiologist, my condition was rapidly getting worse. Without surgery I was looking at congestive heart failure and my premature demise.)

I'm extremely thankful to have gone through this at a time in history when medical science can ensure a high chance of success.

I consider myself very fortunate to have insurance, especially when the first bill alone came to over $200,000.

I'm immensely appreciative of the skilled team of surgeons who carried out the operation.

And I'm beyond grateful to have a partner who has been with me every step of the way, and for all my friends, family, and clients who have showered me with love and healing energy.

I'm a very fortunate man. And I think about how different all this would have been a hundred years ago.

Working with past lives, I'm continually reminded of just how fortunate most of us are. Few of our past lives have been perfect. Most have been spent in poverty.

The majority of them have been lived in circumstances we'd consider primitive by today's standards. As the spirit guides point out, "From your soul's point of view, this may be your best life ever."

I'm sure your life has been full of challenges and disappointments, and the spirit guides wouldn't disagree. With school shootings, homophobic and racist violence, and other threats to safety, the modern world can be a dangerous place.

But when you put things in perspective, most of us in the 21st Century "first world" have a lot to be thankful for.

If you've managed to escape war this time, either as a combatant or a civilian victim, your soul will consider that a true blessing. It will appreciate having the opportunity to complete its life plan without suffering untimely death in an armed conflict.

Have you had surgery in this life? Imagine what your soul has been through in the past. Every one of us will have had amputations, tooth extractions, Caesarian sections, and other medical procedures in previous lifetimes. And, until recently, it would have all been done without anesthetics—often with little expectation of recovery.

If you've given birth successfully in this life, consider yourself lucky. Going back even a hundred years, not only did an appalling number of babies die, but mothers as well. In my sessions, I've seen dozens of cases of women who died from postpartum infections or what was sometimes referred to as childbed fever.

Give thanks if you have a comfortable home. Many of your past lives have been spent in residences that were freezing in winter, or where the smoke from the fireplace would force you to sleep sitting up, or where fleas, lice, bed bugs and rodents would prevent you getting a good night's sleep, sitting up or otherwise.

Be grateful for luxuries like the eight-hour workday, social security, welfare, child-labor laws, the end of slavery, and running water.

In your past lives, losing your spouse, your job, or your eyesight might easily have led to a life of prostitution or having to beg on the streets to survive.

Your soul will appreciate the education you've had, or are,

perhaps, still enjoying in this life. And if you like to read at night, think about how hard that used to be, squinting at the printed page under the light of a sputtering tallow candle (if you were fortunate enough to have a book—or a candle—or to even know how to read).

Take a moment to appreciate, too, how much personal freedom you have. At some point in your many incarnations, you'll have ended up being imprisoned for what might now be considered a trivial crime.

IN A ROOM OF A HUNDRED PEOPLE...

Most of my clients who've had a past life as a prisoner will give prisons a wide birth. Some, however, will be drawn to them, perhaps as a counselor, to help balance karma.

Caroline's past-life trauma was the result of being locked up in a religious institution. Her captors were the nuns who ran the orphanage there.

I said, "I bet you won't ever visit Alcatraz."

She replied, "I've been there seven times."

Though this might seem excessive, it's simply an example of how we're often drawn to places, and even people, to help understand our past.

In a room of a hundred people, how many have visited Alcatraz seven times? I suggest that Caroline would be the one.

You've had lives in which you couldn't marry without your parents' permission, leave the house without your husband's approval, or get a divorce without the church deciding the matter for you. (With gay marriage still being banned in many parts of the world, it's clear we still have a long way to go.)

This life may not be perfect, but if you've made it through childhood without succumbing to polio or measles, have an education, were able to choose your own spouse, and found work you like, then you're doing well. Probably better than you've done in centuries.

So, the next time you grumble about the internet being slow, or the supermarket being out of gluten-free bread, take a moment: Close your eyes, picture yourself having a molar removed without anesthetic in a Medieval marketplace, then open your eyes and say to yourself, "This might be my best life ever!"

SPIRITUAL ACTS

For someone else, this life may not be the best ever—or anything approaching it. Everywhere you look, you'll see signs of suffering, persecution, and injustice. When you see people struggling to make it, how should you respond?

The answer is simple. We're all meant to support one another. It's how we were back in the tribe, and it's how we should be now. To reach out to a fellow soul in need is considered a spiritual act.

Spiritual acts are the things you do to help those who suffer as you once did. Your soul knows what it's like to go to bed hungry every night. It's done that more than once. And when it sees someone going hungry now, it's reminded of its own experience, even if it happened thousands of years ago.

It's important to recognize that you are the adult in a world full of younger and less experienced souls. You have a responsibility to stand up for those who are oppressed or powerless, to speak your truth, to respect those of different ethnic origins, gender and sexual orientations, and economic backgrounds, and to do your part in creating a more compassionate world.

The underdogs are just like you. They breathe, they eat, they think. They are souls beneath the skin. And whatever circumstances they happen to be in, you've been there too.

To you, as an old soul, the homeless person on the street corner isn't someone to be ignored or reviled, they're to be pitied and respected. You're meant to look at them and say, "That could be me." This awareness is a nudge from your soul, and it's designed to prompt some kind of action.

STANDING UP FOR WHAT'S RIGHT

To live a truly spiritual life, ignoring injustice and inequality is not an option.

Imagine if Rosa Parks had said, "Maybe I should just move to the back of the bus…"

Or if Gandhi had said, "Who am I to think I can change anything?"

What if Martin Luther King Jr. had said, "Let's not get our hopes up," instead of, "I have a dream"?

As an old soul, it's incumbent upon you to lead the way. To be a truly spiritual being is to take a loving path. That means working in whatever way you can to build a better world for yourself and others.

It means speaking out against injustice. And it means striving (like nine-year old Lola from Chapter Ten, who volunteers at a homeless shelter) to act from a place of love at all times.

You don't have to inspire dramatic social change to make a

difference. You can manifest your old-soul values in simple ways and still fulfill your soul's desire to express love.

We're all in it together. And you, being an old soul, can choose to lend your energy, in whatever way is appropriate for you, to help others. You have total free will, but you should, for example, always treat people with the same courtesy you'd expect from them.

Remembering that every soul is here to learn, you should encourage curiosity and the pursuit of knowledge, and avoid basing your beliefs and behavior on propaganda, superstition, or biased information.

Since no soul is inherently better or worse than any other, you should choose to support equality. That women earn less than men, and people of color are treated more harshly than whites in the judicial system, are injustices no soul should tolerate.

Your soul is motivated to build bridges, not walls. You should do your best to understand another person's point of view.

You've suffered from the effects of terrible injustice in previous incarnations, and even this one. Though life is sometimes terribly unfair, it's your responsibly to help balance injustice and treat others kindly.

In this modern era in which those in power lie with impunity, and checks and balances are constantly under assault, your soul will seek more than ever to redress the imbalance by encouraging you to speak your truth at all times.

Peace is the soul's natural state. Aggression is simply a manifestation of fear. As a fearless old soul, it's essential to take the path of nonviolence and learn to solve disagreements peacefully.

Every soul requires freedom to allow it to fulfill its life plan. Freedom is always a two-way street. What you want for yourself is what others require too: the freedom to be who you are and who you're meant to be.

Love is your soul's ultimate goal, but it's also the path that takes you there. Expressing your authentic, true self means walking the path of love at all times.

This means being loving towards yourself as well as others. Everyone has the right to love and be loved, regardless of sexual orientation, gender, ethnic origin, or beliefs.

And don't worry if you fall down along the way. You're only human. But when you find yourself not living up to these higher values, don't beat yourself up. Simply resolve to do better next time.

Cooperation, respect, knowledge, equality, understanding, justice, truth, peace, freedom, and love are your soul's paths, its goals, and its core values.

Walking the paths helps you reach the goals and, in turn, allows you to embody the core values. It's really quite simple.

EXERCISE: CALIBRATE YOUR OLD SOUL BELIEFS

There are certain beliefs that accompany each of your soul's ten core values. When you're acting in harmony with your soul, these beliefs should resonate with you. Conversely, when you're out of sync with your soul, the beliefs may not resonate so strongly.

In this exercise, there's no wrong or right. Whether or not you relate to a particular belief is not an indicator of your soul's age. We're all walking the paths. It's a process. None of us is perfect.

The aim of this exercise is to help you determine which areas need attention. Alongside each statement, simply determine how strongly you agree, using numbers from 0-10.

- **Cooperation:** Everyone deserves the support of others
- **Respect:** Everyone is worthy of being treated with respect

- **Knowledge:** Everyone should have access to knowledge and education
- **Equality:** Everyone is equal regardless of ethnicity or gender
- **Understanding:** Everyone deserves to be seen and heard
- **Justice:** Everyone should be treated fairly at all times
- **Truth:** Everyone deserves honesty and transparency
- **Peace:** Everyone has a right to live without fear of violence
- **Freedom:** Everyone should have maximum freedom of opportunity
- **Love:** Everyone is worthy of love and compassion

Remember that all your soul's paths are two-way streets. It's your soul's desire to extend the same kindnesses and opportunities to others that you'd wish for yourself. For example, if you agree with the statement, "*I* have a right to live without fear of violence," then it follows that you should agree with the statement, "*Everyone* has a right to live without fear of violence."

If you gave yourself a score of anything other than ten for any one of them, then it's a sign there's something there for you to work on. If you disagree with the statement, "Everyone has a right to live without fear of violence," or any of the others, then spend some time examining why you feel you deserve something that others don't.

We live in a world where the ten core values are not respected, or even understood. In fact, our predominantly young-soul society is a glaring example of what happens when the core values are ignored.

A woman named Tondalao Hall is serving a sentence of 30-to-life in an Oklahoma jail for failure to protect her children, while the man who terrorized her and her children walks free.

And in Florida, a man named Robert Spellman is serving a

20-year sentence for stealing ten cartons of cigarettes. I'm sure you don't need me to point out that the poor and minorities are always the ones getting screwed over by politicians who want to make a name for themselves through tough stances on welfare, immigration, or recreational drugs.

It's not easy, in a world of meanness and insensitivity, to avoid getting angry. And that's okay. You're meant to do that.

Sadly, some of us feel that when we get angry, we've somehow failed a spiritual test. Sure, if you vent your anger by lashing out at your partner or kicking the dog, you've got work to do. But the emotions you feel are designed to instill action and can be channeled into helping those who need it, rather than being internalized.

Your emotions are the voice of your soul. If you're not outraged by the injustice you see in the world around you, then something is wrong. You *should* be outraged. Your soul is trying to get you to do something about it.

If you're not appalled by the greed of Wall Street bankers, or the destruction of the oceans by pollution, or the threat to us all from global warming, nuclear weapons, and the loss of drinkable water, then it's time to pay attention. Disinterest and complacency are the prerogative of the privileged.

You're the old soul—the adult in the room. You have significant responsibilities. You have to lead the way. Speak out against injustice, stand up for what you believe in, and make sure you're on the right side of history as you approach the end of your soul's long, heroic odyssey.

EPILOGUE

JOURNEY'S END

*A*t the completion of this incarnation, your soul will leave the body of which it has been an integral part and, as it has done many times before, make its way back to the Astral Plane, its spiritual home.

The first thing it will do when it gets there is to review the life that just ended. Only after undergoing this often emotionally grueling experience will your soul truly understand all the lessons learned during its time on earth.

During the review, your soul will relive the memories of the life it just completed. It will remember every conversation it was ever involved in. It will revisit all the interactions it had with others. And it will do so in a split second. (It's why people who've had a near death experience will often say, "My entire life flashed in front of my eyes." They're describing the first part of the review.)

Next, your soul will experience all the emotions associated with the life it just had. It will not only feel its own emotions, but that of others, too.

By feeling the joys, hurts, and everything else your behavior inspired in those you encountered during your time on earth, your soul can truly understand the degree to which its life was a success.

Almost as soon as your soul gets to the Astral Plane, it will begin planning for its next incarnation. It will look for lessons still to be learned, new places to be investigated, and a soul family to share the journey.

For an old soul like you, the voyage from your first incarnation to now has taken you from the Neolithic era to the Space Age.

During this time, you've investigated lives on all the inhabitable continents. You've learned skills like fishing, hunting, masonry, and medicine, studied literature in scores of languages, and explored new frontiers to satisfy your soul's innate curiosity and thirst for knowledge.

Everything you've experienced has taken you closer to embodying peace, truth, love, and the other higher values to which all souls aspire. At some point in the future, however, your soul will assess all the lessons learned and decide it's time to leave the Physical Plane for good. It will have no regrets, just a sense of completion.

Few old souls fear actually dying. Having gone through the transition from the Physical to the Astral Plane so many times before, your soul will have lost its fear of death itself. It may fear a certain kind of death. If you drowned in a recent past life, for example, it might strongly prefer not to go the same way again.

One thing's for sure—when you reach the end of your final incarnation, your soul will actually look forward to no longer having to reincarnate on the Physical Plane.

When I tell a very old soul this might well be their last incarnation, their reaction is usually something like, "That makes me so happy! I just want to go home." Being so close to the end, they can feel the emotions associated with being in spirit again.

THE EXPERIENCE IS NOT THE LESSON

Always remember that the experience is not the lesson. The lesson is what you draw from the experience. And there's always an empowering lesson from every experience.

When you review your life, you'll look for the lessons you can take away from all that happened to you while you were incarnate. But you don't have to wait till you're dead to do that. You can do it now.

Your soul is all about growth. It's prime directive, after all, is to evolve. And you can radically speed up your personal evolution by processing your life as you go along. The most important thing is to find the positive lessons from all that happens to you.

Journaling helps you process your life as you go along. It's a form of therapy, allowing you to come to conclusions about events in your life that otherwise remain as thoughts. It's a way, too, of freeing up your mental hard-drive and letting your spirit guides in.

Though there are always powerful lessons to be drawn from the traumatic events of your life, your soul grows fastest through joy. Your soul wants to be happy. Which is one reason that my spirit guides so often remind people I work with about the importance of lightening up.

Two partners in a small company once asked me for ideas on how to improve their business. To everyone's amusement, the spirit guides' first suggestion was to end each week by going bowling. There was a deeper purpose to this, of course. Bowling is fun, and that would help their relationship. And by getting out of their left brains and more into their bodies, they'd actually be able to better process the events of the preceding week.

We're here to enjoy life. So, if you like bowling, make sure you do it. The same goes for anything you love to do. Make sure you're doing it. Once, after looking at a client's life plan, I asked, "Why are you not acting?" She replied, "I don't know. I love doing it!" Needless to say, she was a Performer type with multiple lives as an actor in her soul's recent past lives.

As my spirit guides frequently say, "You don't want to be 100 years old and saying, 'I wish I'd danced more.'" But, whatever you love—whether it's travel, opera, soccer, writing, good food, or hiking—then make sure you're doing it while you're here.

A SUCCESSFUL LIFE

What happens if you screw up this life badly? The spirit guides say there are no mistakes, just choices with different consequences. If things don't work out according to plan, you'll always get another chance. That's why we reincarnate.

Often, when I tell someone about a past life they'll say, "But that's my life now," or, "Are we talking about this life or the past life?" When your soul fails to complete its life plan, it will choose similar opportunities in its next incarnation. The location and circumstances of the next life might seem very different, but they'll be designed to teach you the lessons you missed out on. It's like failing an exam in calculus. You'll have to take the exam again, but it may not be identical to the one you took before.

What is a successful life? It's one in which you completed your life plan with a minimum of interruption and dealt with all the major lessons you chose as part of your life plan. The key to having a truly successful life is to know what your soul seeks from being here. It begins with understanding who you are, since who you are reveals so much about why you're here.

A successful life is one in which you created little or no negative karma (meaning you didn't do anything to interfere with another soul's ability to complete their life plan). But it's also one in which you created positive karma by helping others to live their lives successfully.

When you get to the Astral Plane, you want to be able to say, "I gave it my best." How do you know when you're giving it your best? Your soul will tell you. The soul is always fulfilled when you're on the right path. And your emotions are the voice of your soul. If you feel happy and content in a situation, that's usually a sign that you're on the right track.

If you get derailed, then your soul will sound the alarm and try to get you back on the right path. Sometimes it's just a feeling that things are not quite right or could be better. Other times, it can be a constant sense of dissatisfaction or even outright distress. Such emotions are designed to inspire change and not to be ignored.

When this life is over, how can you tell if you've done a good job? If you were kind and considerate—despite everything the Physical Plane threw at you—if you made an effort to not deliberately hurt anyone out of malice, and if you can say that you tried to do what was best for yourself and others, then it's a job well done.

THE LEGACY YOU LEAVE

Maya Angelou once said, "I would like to be known as an intelligent woman, a courageous woman, a loving woman, a woman who teaches by being."

Do you and your family still talk about Great Grandma, or is there someone amongst your ancestors whose name still comes up, decades or longer after they passed over to the other side?

What do you want people to say about you when you're gone? That you stuck it out until retirement in a job you never really liked, or that you followed your dreams and helped to leave the world a better a place? Wouldn't you prefer to be the inspirational person the family still talks about generations from now?

You can't control what people say about you. Or can you? What people remember about you is within your power to create. How much better would it be to have them describe you as an ass-kicking force of nature, a beautiful heart, or a person who lived a really full life—than unremarkable, selfish, or that you never really did anything?

You have the free will that allows you to make choices about how others see you. In this life, you might find you have the opportunity to touch the hearts and minds of millions. But even if it's in your life plan to be mostly alone, it's unlikely you live in a complete vacuum, unable to influence anyone.

You have a choice when it comes to what you give to others. I'm sure you'd agree it would be so much better to be remembered for your generosity of spirit than as someone who was penny-pinching and miserly.

You have a choice whether to be a trusted friend and family member or someone who consistently let others down. I'm sure you'd prefer to be remembered as having been loyal.

You have a choice when it comes to opening your heart. Do you want to be remembered as a loving presence who made people feel cared for or as someone who was emotionally shut down or distant?

You have a choice when it comes to being with others. You might prefer to be remembered as someone who had friends and meaningful relationships than as the person who was always the outsider.

You have a choice around expressing your truth. It might seem safer to hide your opinions or not say what's on your mind. But wouldn't you prefer to be remembered for expressing yourself openly and confidently?

You have a choice when it comes to how you behave toward those less fortunate than you. Wouldn't you like to be remembered as someone who treated everyone as an equal and who stood up for others?

You have a choice around how you express your self-worth. I'm sure you'd much rather be remembered as someone who expressed inner confidence rather than as a person who was jealous or insecure?

You have a choice in whether you will be remembered as never being able to stand up for yourself or as an empowered person who helped empower others.

You have a choice in whether future generations remember you as the person who seized opportunities when they came your way or as someone who let fear prevent them from taking risks and never fulfilled their potential.

And you have a choice in whether you're remembered for having taken responsibility for the choices you made or for having let others make decisions for you.

Think about who you have the potential to be. When you review your life on the Astral Plane, your soul will not calculate the value of the life you just had by the number of TV shows you watched. But if you volunteered at a soup kitchen to feed those less fortunate than yourself, or you created beautiful art to inspire and give value to others' lives, then that's what will truly matter. And that's what those you leave behind will care about.

How do you want to be remembered? Here's an exercise to give you some control over your reputation.

EXERCISE: WRITE YOUR WIKIPEDIA PAGE

Put yourself a few years in the future. Five is perfect, but sooner is fine, too. How do you want your Wikipedia entry to read? (And don't worry! This is just an exercise. Not every soul is here to be in the public eye.) Don't micromanage your future! Two or three paragraphs should be enough.

- What do you want others to know about you?
- What have been your notable achievements?
- What are you still planning to do in the future?

Now think about the things you can do now that will lead to you being the person you described, and then start planning the steps you'll take to get there. Let your Wiki page be a guiding light as you move forward.

GOING TOWARDS THE LIGHT

Do you have to be perfect before leaving this world? Thankfully, no—otherwise we'd all be stuck here indefinitely.

Perfection is not the goal. It's simply to get to a point where everything your soul wanted to learn has been learned.

It's enough that you feel you have a strong grasp of what it means to be kind and compassionate and loving, and to have evolved beyond a state of fear.

Eventually, your soul will be done with life on Earth. That's when it will begin the last part of its journey—one that will take it back to the Universal Consciousness of which it was once a part.

Most of us need somewhere between 100 and 120 lifetimes before we reach a point where we can finally stop reincarnating.

You'll have a sense of this on the Physical Plane and will usually feel that you've quite simply had enough of being here—not in a suicidal or depressive way—but more of a feeling that you've been around the block enough times.

You can't be absolutely certain this is your last life until you process everything that happened during your review on the Astral Plane. Only then can you tell whether there's sufficient reason to return to Earth once more, or if it's time to call it good.

WHERE DO OLD SOULS GO?

When all your lives are completed, you'll no longer come back to this world. That doesn't mean you'll rest on your laurels in some kind of spiritual senior center. You'll still have work to do.

The next stage of your journey will involve being a spirit guide for members of your soul family who are still going through the cycle of life and death in the physical world. This could take some time.

You'll be on the Astral Plane until the very last member of your soul family, that group of souls who first incarnated with you thousands of years ago, finally makes it over to the other side for the last time.

Will you miss being human? Although your soul has a huge vested interest in the successful outcome of each incarnation, once it no longer has to come back, it will have no regrets. It will, instead, feel a sense of total completion.

It will lose any emotional connection to life in the physical dimension, as long as it feels that its experience is complete.

After your soul has been on the Astral Plane for a while (months or years in our way of measuring time), it will lose the personality it most recently had.

Your soul will still retain some awareness of its individuality until it moves, in the company of the entire family, to the next level of consciousness: the Causal Plane.

Once back on the Causal Plane, the dimension where your journey began, you'll gain a far greater sense of unity. You'll see yourself as an individual component of a higher and loving consciousness.

This consciousness will act as spirit guides to others still on the Astral and Physical Planes.

After the Causal Plane interval, your soul will merge, to once again become part of the Universal Consciousness.

THE SEARCH FOR BELONGING

The older your soul becomes, the more it seeks out others of a similar age.

But it can be hard to find a community in which you can explore your spiritual old-soul purpose without fear of rejection or ridicule.

The is one of the main reasons I created the Soul World membership program—a virtual gathering place where old souls can explore the teachings of my spirit guides, and do so in the company of kindred spirits.

At the deepest level of who you are, when you strip away the fears, the uncertainties, and the limiting beliefs, there lies your soul. And your soul is all-loving. It's a small piece of a vast and endlessly loving universe.

While you're still here in this plane of existence, I encourage you to be the loving person you are at your soul's core, traveling through this world as a beacon of old-soul values.

Live your life with kindness and compassion.

Treat others with the respect and honesty you'd want for yourself.

Dance, sing, bake, hike, or do whatever your heart and soul desire.

Be someone others admire.

Make this life count.

Make it your best incarnation ever.

And, as you continue to move forward through this particular lifetime, my desire is that The Old Soul's Guidebook will help you to navigate the Physical Plane with an empowering sense of who you are, why you're here, and what choices are in your highest interest at all times.

May you love and be loved, and when this incarnation is over, may you be remembered as the inspirational old soul others aspire to be.

The more you examine your life, the easier it will become to make choices that are in your highest interest and are consistent with your soul's life plan. Remember that the experience is not the lesson. The lesson is what you draw from the experience. We support you at all times in achieving everything your soul desires in this life, and we remind you that knowing who you are is the key to knowing why you're here. Your destiny is not a secret, and it's our purpose to offer clarity and guidance to help you on your soul's journey.

— AINSLIE MACLEOD'S SPIRIT GUIDES

APPENDIX A

HOW TO EXPLORE PAST LIVES
WITH ME

What is past-life regression and why should you care? Put simply, a past-life regression is when you revisit a traumatic event from a prior incarnation to create healing in this life.

By reminding your soul that whatever awful things happened to it are from another lifetime, not this, you allow it to release the fears, blocks, and limiting beliefs that interfere with your ability to fully live the life your soul intended.

One of the monthly benefits in my Soul World membership program includes a past-life regression, after which Christine and I help participants process their experience. If—like me— you're one of those impatient types, you may be pleased to know that my regressions are not just effective, they're fast!

For more information about past-life regressions, and all the benefits available in the Soul World membership program, visit soulworld.com

THE TEN SOUL TYPES

1. **Helper:** Of Service, Practical, Passive
2. **Caregiver:** Nurturing, Empathic, Prone to Self-Neglect
3. **Educator:** Informative, Eloquent, Verbose
4. **Thinker:** Rational, Curious, Over-Analytical
5. **Creator:** Sensitive, Creative, Ungrounded
6. **Performer:** Communicative, Playful, Pretentious
7. **Hunter:** Physical, Task-Oriented, Inflexible
8. **Leader:** Charismatic, Active, Intransigent
9. **Spiritualist:** Compassionate, Spiritual/Religious, Obsessive
10. **Transformer:** Inspirational, Motivational, Unworldly

PAST-LIFE FEARS

1. **The Fear of Loss** is the result of losing loved ones, your home, or your money in a past life. It creates uncertainty about the future.
2. **The Fear of Betrayal** is caused by infidelity or disloyalty in a past life. It shows up as mistrust of certain people.
3. **The Fear of Intimacy** is related to emotional suffering in a past life. It causes a reluctance to open your heart.
4. **The Fear of Rejection** is the result of abandonment in a past life. It can show up as a tendency to isolate or not belong.
5. **The Fear of Self-Expression** is caused by persecution for your beliefs in a past life. It creates challenges in speaking your truth.
6. **The Fear of Authority** stems from being abused by authority in a past life. It will cause you to identify with the underdog.
7. **The Fear of Inferiority** is the result of being treated

with disdain in a past life. It will show up as low self-esteem.

8. **The Fear of Powerlessness** is caused by slavery or imprisonment in a past life. It will cause you to resist being told what to do.

9. **The Fear of Failure** is related to a disappointing or incomplete past life. It creates a lack of belief in your potential for success.

10. **The Fear of Death** is the result of having caused the death of others in a past life. It shows up as a heightened responsibility for others.

ACKNOWLEDGMENTS

I'm deeply grateful to my talented old-soul friends Kat Eggleston for her editing expertise, Dev Darshan for her inspiring copywriting, and Shelly Francis for not only helping me navigate the world of independent publishing, but also her support in shaping the final product.

I'm truly indebted to my amazing clients who have been so willing to allow me to share their stories, and to my spirit guides without whom there would be no book.

I extend my heartfelt thanks to Oprah Winfrey for her help in getting my work out into the world.

And to my wife, Christine, I'd like to express my utmost gratitude for your unwavering support, wisdom, and love.

ABOUT THE AUTHOR

Through his books, workshops, retreats, Soul World membership program, and private readings—spiritual teacher, author, and past-life psychic Ainslie MacLeod has taken thousands of people on a journey into the world of the soul to discover their life's purpose.

Working with elevated spirit guides, Ainslie acts as a direct conduit between this plane and the Spiritual Universe, offering information designed to inspire, illuminate, and empower.

He has written two previous books, *The Instruction* and *The Transformation*, and has been a featured guest on Oprah's Soul Series and her SuperSoul Conversations.

Ainslie is a faculty member at the Kripalu Center, and was the recipient of a gold medal for his first book, *The Instruction*, from the Independent Publisher Association. He lives on a tranquil island in the Pacific Northwest.

Visit him online at ainsliemacleod.com and soulworld.com.

ABOUT SOUL WORLD PRESS

SOUL WORLD PRESS®
SEATTLE

Soul World Press exists to support readers in living the life their soul intended. We believe that when people recognize the continuity of their soul's growth across lifetimes, they can tap into their current life purpose with more ease and joy.

Connect with our online community at SoulWorld.com.

CPSIA information can be obtained
at www.ICGtesting.com
Printed in the USA
LVHW091648020222
710068LV00007B/650

9 781732 925502